Fodor's
25 Best

SYDNEY

How to Use
This Book

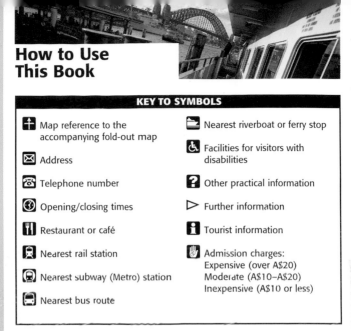

KEY TO SYMBOLS	
✚ Map reference to the accompanying fold-out map	⛴ Nearest riverboat or ferry stop
✉ Address	♿ Facilities for visitors with disabilities
☎ Telephone number	❷ Other practical information
🕐 Opening/closing times	▷ Further information
🍴 Restaurant or café	ℹ Tourist information
🚆 Nearest rail station	✋ Admission charges: Expensive (over A$20) Moderate (A$10–A$20) Inexpensive (A$10 or less)
🚇 Nearest subway (Metro) station	
🚌 Nearest bus route	

This guide is divided into four sections
● Essential Sydney: An introduction to the city and tips on making the most of your stay.
● Sydney by Area: We've broken the city into five areas, and recommended the best sights, shops, entertainment venues, nightlife and restaurants in each one. Suggested walks help you to explore on foot.
● Where to Stay: The best hotels, whether you're looking for luxury, budget or something in between.
● Need to Know: The info you need to make your trip run smoothly, including getting about by public transport, weather tips, emergency phone numbers and useful websites.

Navigation In the Sydney by Area chapter, we've given each area its own color, which is also used on the locator maps throughout the book and the map on the inside front cover.

Maps The fold-out map with this book is a comprehensive street plan of Sydney. The grid on this fold-out map is the same as the grid on the locator maps within the book. We've given grid references within the book for each sight and listing.

Contents

Introducing Sydney

Cosmopolitan, diverse, energetic and easygoing, Sydney has colonial heritage, dazzling modern buildings and a free-wheeling lifestyle. Its iconic, sheltered port and sunny, subtropical climate help make it a major tourist destination.

Sydney is clean, unpolluted and relatively safe, and it's not surprising that it is most often voted as one of the world's most liveable cities. But, far from being the clichéd sun, sand, surf and sport scene you might expect, Sydney also has world-class museums and galleries as well as a roster of shops that include branches of luxury brands and boutique local designers. The cuisine is truly superb––Sydney is now one of the modern food capitals of the world—and don't forget the wine.

After dark you can take in an opera or ballet at the Sydney Opera House, see a first-class theatrical production, dance the night away in a classy pub, take in the sparkling vistas from a vantage point such as Sydney Tower, or spend the evening sampling local beer in a historic sandstone hotel at Sydney's birthplace, The Rocks.

A vibrant world business capital, Sydney has a commercial buzz that permeates the Central Business District (CBD). The city embraces people of all races and nationalities and, although this doesn't make it a multicultural utopia, you feel you are visiting an international destination. An Asian presence is strong, and you'll overhear any number of European languages.

The pace in Sydney is faster than in other parts of Australia, and the nasally Australian English, with its distinctive colloquialisms, is delivered double time. The often-heard expressions "No worries, mate" and "She'll be right" say much about the attitudes here. Come to Sydney with an open mind, meet people halfway, take the city as it comes, and you're bound to have a relaxing and thoroughly good time.

FACTS AND FIGURES

- From 1,400 people in 1788, Sydney's population has grown to more than 5.1 million people.
- Around 70 percent of Sydneysiders are a combination of at least two ethnic backgrounds, while 40 percent are foreign-born.
- Every day approximately 615,000 people, including residents and visitors, come into Sydney for work or leisure.

FAMOUS SYDNEYSIDERS

Heading overseas to hit the big time is an Australian tradition. Among Sydney's most famous exports are supermodel Elle Macpherson, actors Mel Gibson and Cate Blanchett, author and TV personality Clive James, and art critic Robert Hughes. Although actress Nicole Kidman left her place of birth, Hawaii, at four years, she considers herself an honorary Sydneysider.

THE DIASPORA

Nearly one million Australians—5 percent of the population—live and/or work in other countries. These people have been quiet achievers in Asian countries such as Singapore and China for many years. The diaspora actually promotes Australia's commercial interests, and when these people return, they bring new skills and new experiences to the workplace.

ABORIGINAL PRESENCE

Aboriginal peoples have lived in Australia for more than 60,000 years and many of their descendants live in Sydney. The vestiges of Aboriginal culture in Sydney consist of shell middens on the Harbour foreshores, rock carvings in the surrounding national parks, and in place names such as Woolloomooloo, Turramurra and Parramatta.

A Short Stay in Sydney

DAY 1

Morning Have an early breakfast and walk to the **Royal Botanic Garden Sydney** (▷ 24–25) for a quiet stroll around the grounds. You might detour to Mrs Macquarie's Point from where you have a classic vista of the **Sydney Opera House** (▷ 30–31) and **Sydney Harbour Bridge** (▷ 27).

Mid-morning Hop on a ferry for a tour of the Harbour. You could go to **Taronga Zoo** (▷ 32–33), or take the public ferry to **Manly** (▷ 95) and head for Manly Beach via the lively Corso Boulevard.

Lunch Have lunch on the Manly Wharf or take the ferry back to **Circular Quay** (▷ 46) and catch a bus along George Street to **Chinatown** (▷ 58) for a meal. The streets around here are worth exploring for interesting Asian curios and exotic food ingredients.

Afternoon After a look around Chinatown, take a walk to **Darling Harbour** (▷ 60–61) and view the marine exhibits at **Sea Life Sydney Aquarium** (▷ 60–61) before heading to the **Australian Maritime Museum** (▷ 56–57) via the Harbourside shopping complex.

Dinner Take the Light Rail and venture back into the CBD. Here you'll find an array of dining options, some with city views. If you are looking for budget meals, try one of the excellent food courts in the big retail complexes here.

Evening Take in a performance at the **Opera House** (▷ 30–31) where you can choose from a range of opera, musical and drama performances. Be sure to walk around the Harbour foreshore afterward for stunning city and Harbour views.

DAY 2

Morning Walk from Circular Quay to **The Rocks** (▷ 43), with its shops and galleries, restaurants and pubs. You could stop for a look at the **Museum of Contemporary Art** (▷ 40–41) or continue to the BridgeClimb terminus for a morning climb on the **Sydney Harbour Bridge** (▷ 27).

Mid-morning Walk to the elegant **Queen Victoria Building** (▷ 80) where you can shop for brand-name clothing and quality souvenirs. There are plenty of dining options here, but tea and scones at the Palace Tea Rooms certainly suits the setting.

Lunch Head to **David Jones Food Hall** (▷ 84) for a picnic lunch to have in **Hyde Park** (▷ 80). Afterward walk to Macquarie Street to see the **Hyde Park Barracks** (▷ 75), where you'll get a feeling for Sydney's convict past. Opposite is historic St. James Church, dating from 1824.

Afternoon Then walk down Macquarie Street past **State Parliament House** (▷ 82) and the **State Library** (▷ 82) to **Circular Quay** (▷ 46) for a coffee. You may have time to divert into the **Royal Botanic Garden Sydney** (▷ 24–25) for a stroll through this amazing plant collection.

Dinner Dine on sweeping Harbour views and contemporary Australian fare at Café Sydney at the **Customs House** (▷ 46), then stroll to The Rocks nearby. The narrow streets here evoke the character of old Sydney Town and there are several interesting old pubs.

Evening There are some great nightspots around the city, but why not double down on those views by heading for cocktails on the 36th floor of the Shangri-La Hotel at the **Blu Bar on 36** (▷ 50).

▼▼▼ **Art Gallery of New South Wales** ▷ **70–71** Contains some of Australia's most admired works of art.

Australian Maritime Museum ▷ **56–57** The nation's marine history and a moored submarine.

Australian Museum ▷ **72–73** An excellent collection of cultural and scientific exhibits.

Bondi Beach ▷ **94** This crescent of sandy beach is a popular hot summer's day destination.

Chinese Garden of Friendship and Chinatown ▷ **58** Sydney's vibrant Asian core.

City Centre ▷ **74** The energetic business hub of Australia is also a retail and dining mecca.

Hyde Park Barracks ▷ **75** Shows what transportees experienced in the early days.

Manly ▷ **95** Explore the Northern Beaches and vibrant beachside precinct.

Museum of Contemporary Art ▷ **40–41** Cutting-edge contemporary art.

Museum of Sydney ▷ **42** Sydney's past, well displayed in intimate galleries.

Paddington ▷ **76–77** Walk the backstreets in this suburb of terraced houses.

Powerhouse Museum ▷ **59** One of Australia's best collections of technology and decorative arts can be found here.

The Rocks ▷ **43** Sydney's birthplace, with its old architecture, is well worth exploring.

Royal Botanic Garden Sydney and the Domain ▷ **24–25** Stroll here and have a picnic.

Royal National Park ▷ **96** A wonderland of rainforests, beaches and coastal walking trails.

Sea Life Sydney Aquarium and Darling Harbour ▷ **60–61** Sharks, rays and more from the Great Barrier Reef.

Sydney Harbour ▷ **26** The iconic focal point of the city and the reference point for all attractions.

Sydney Harbour Bridge ▼▼▼ ▷ **27** Climb this icon for 360-degree views of the city—then tell your friends.

Sydney Harbour National Park ▷ **28–29** This collection of reserves are accessible by ferry.

Sydney Observatory ▷ **44–45** A working observatory that doubles as a museum of astronomy.

Sydney Olympic Park ▷ **97** Home of the 2000 Olympics and a focal point for sports of all kinds.

Sydney Opera House ▷ **30–31** This world architectural icon is the hub of Sydney's performance arts.

Sydney Tower and Skywalk ▷ **78** Come on a fine day for the views, stay for a meal, and dare to take the Skywalk experience.

Taronga Zoo ▷ **32–33** Home to the full range of Australia's wildlife, plus views of the Harbour and the CBD.

Vaucluse House and Vaucluse ▷ **98–99** Heritage-listed mansion, set in well-tended gardens.

These pages are a quick guide to the Top 25, which are described in more detail later. Here they are listed alphabetically, and the tinted background shows which area they are in.

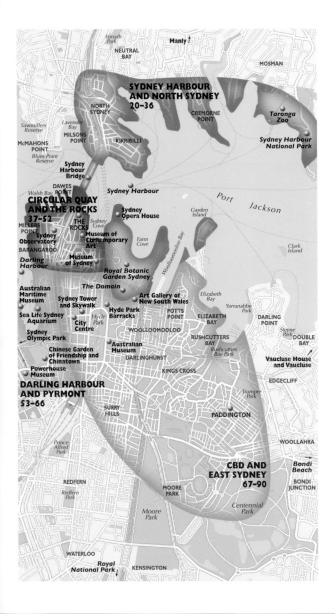

Shopping

Apart from having the usual roster of international brand-name retail outlets, Sydney has many shops selling designer clothing, original arts and crafts and stunning gemstone jewelry.

A Memento

Visitors keen to take home a classic memento tend to go for an item of Australiana such as opal or pearl jewelry, kangaroo or crocodile leather products or exquisite craft objects in glass, wood, porcelain and silver inspired by Australian nature. Australian-made skincare, homeware, wines and gourmet items are also very popular.

Aussie Wares

The range of Aboriginal arts and crafts is enormous. But try to distinguish between handmade craft items from Aboriginal settlements and the mundane, generic goods that are mass produced and have no authenticity. Look out for the signed traditional bowls, didgeridoos, boomerangs and wood carvings. Art enthusiasts go for the Arnhem Land bark paintings and Central Australian dot paintings. Seek out a reputable gallery and ask questions regarding provenance and authenticity. Original Australian design brands to look out for include the wildly colored Romance Was Born, the winsome Zimmerman, Dinosaur Designs and Mambo, with surf and streetwear featuring funky designs. There are several local store chains selling goods that are not found internationally, including the Australian Geographic

There are plenty of shopping opportunities in Sydney's individual shops, shopping malls and arcades

---

MUSEUM SHOPS

At the Art Gallery of New South Wales (▷ 70–71), you'll find Sydney's best selection of art books and cards. The Museum of Contemporary Art (▷ 40–41) offers jewelry, design objects and books inspired by Australian designers. The shop at the Australian Museum (▷ 72–73) focuses on Australian nature books. The Australian Centre for Photography (▷ 79) showcases local talent.

Shop (▷ 104), offering environmentally friendly goods, Australian nature books and outdoor clothing. The Object Shop (▷ 86), located at the Australian Design Centre, showcases handmade craft and design pieces from local artisans.

Food and Drink

Those who have sampled the widely exported Aussie wines will be impressed by the huge range on offer. Australia's wine-growing regions offer some spectacular products, from Margaret River chardonnay to Clare Valley riesling, Heathcote shiraz and cool climate sparkling wine, such as Ninth Island and Arras, from Tasmania. Finally, if you want to impress friends back home with an item not found elsewhere, pick up a macadamia nut cracker. Normally sold with a bunch of nuts to crack, this threaded screw device cracks the shells of Australia's major contribution to the world's food stocks. The best place in the city to sample Australian foods is in the lower ground-floor food hall of the David Jones department store in Market Street (▷ 84). Here you'll find a wonderful selection of produce including delicatessen lines, Aussie wines and beers, cheeses, meats, seafood, fruits and vegetables.

AUSTRALIAN GEMS AND JEWELRY

Sydney is internationally renowned for the range and quality of its opal, pearl and other gemstone jewelry. The best jewelry shops feature original designs utilizing multi-colored opals, lustrous South Sea pearls and exquisite Argyle diamonds in white, pink and champagne shades. You can also buy loose stones, especially opals; the high-quality Australian varieties are recognized as some of the best in the world. You can purchase gemstones and jewelry tax free. The value of an opal is judged by the depth of hue. Red is the most prized, followed by orange, yellow, green, blue, indigo and violet. Buy only solid opals, not inferior doublets or triplets. South Sea pearls are graded by luster, tone, size, shape, surface perfection and rarity.

Shopping by Theme

Whether you're looking for a shopping mall, a quirky market or a designer boutique, you'll find it all in Sydney. On this page, shops are listed by theme. For a more detailed write-up, see the page listed.

Sydney by Night

Restaurants offering alfresco dining, bars with spectacular views and nightclubs that stay open late keep Sydney lively after dark. A huge influx of immigrants in the last few years has energized the restaurant scene as well.

The Music Scene and More
The area from Circular Quay (▷ 46) to the Sydney Opera House (▷ 30–31) bustles at night; Newtown, Darlinghurst and Paddington have the hippest nightclubs, pubs and bars; and Surry Hills, Enmore and Erskineville have plenty of pubs hosting live music.

Take in the Lights
Take the elevator to the observation deck of Sydney Tower, called Sydney Tower Eye (▷ 78; last entry 8pm), for a glittering panorama of Sydney Harbour (▷ 26) and the city, or take a meal in one of the revolving restaurants. Even when the tower is closed, it's worth your while to take in the views from the adjoining park. Walk down the hill for dinner in Chinatown (▷ 58).

Drink with a View
Relax with a cocktail as you take in the view from the 36th floor in the Shangri-la Hotel (▷ 112). Or head for the Hacienda Sydney above Circular Quay at the Pullman Quay Grand Sydney Harbour (61 Macquarie Street). Come here for cocktails, Cuban food and a 1950s Miami vibe. When hunger strikes, consider Quay (▷ 52) on the Upper Level of the Overseas Passenger Terminal, one of Sydney's finest restaurants, or watch the harbor sparkle at sunset at the waterside Opera Bar.

Bright lights and fabulous views—Sydney by night

ON THE WATER AND DANCING
Take a night cruise of Sydney Harbour aboard the *John Cadman*. Captain Cook Cruises (☎ 9206 1122) offers a three-course à la carte menu as you pass well-known city landmarks. The tour includes entertainment and dancing.

Where to Eat

Sydney is such a multicultural city that it's not surprising to find food from all corners of the globe within a radius of a few miles. Food courts in shopping malls are often a tempting medley of the world's cuisines.

What's on the Menu?

Sydney, one of the world's culinary capitals, is home to many chefs with a worldwide reputation. Modern Australian cuisine, which fuses European and Asian food styles with local ingredients, is now a distinct cuisine. Dishes incorporating Aboriginal foods containing bush tucker ingredients, such as kangaroo, emu, crocodile and native fruits and nuts, have been added to the menu. Asian restaurants are everywhere; they include world-class Chinese, along with refined dishes from Indonesia, India, Taiwan, Korea and Vietnam. Seafood plays a large role in Sydney menus and local specialties include Sydney rock oysters, kingfish, enormous prawns, scallops and squid. Many seafood restaurants have waterfront locations, where you can buy excellent fish-and-chips to take out—Bondi Beach (▷ 94), Circular Quay (▷ 46) and Manly (▷ 95) are good spots for alfresco dining.

Sydney's Budget Restaurants

Sydney has many cafés and budget restaurants that are BYO (bring your own alcohol). Apart from the many food courts, you can find good budget eats in areas such as Oxford Street in Paddington, Crown Street in Surry Hills, Enmore Road in Enmore, King Street in Newtown, Glebe Point Road in Glebe, and Chinatown.

WINES OF NEW SOUTH WALES

There are 14 different wine regions in New South Wales. Hunter Valley wines, exported to Europe, the US and Asia, are worth seeking out. The state's varied landscape affords a great range of vineyards, from coastal to cool climate. Excellent winemakers include Lerida Estate, Brangayne, Bago and Crooked River.

The pick of the ocean in Sydney's beachside restaurants

Where to Eat by Cuisine

There are places to eat to suit all tastes and budgets in Sydney. On this page, they are listed by cuisine. For a more detailed description of each venue, see the page listed.

Australian
360 Bar and Dining (▷ 89)
Aria (▷ 51)
The Bach Eatery (▷ 106)
Bistro Moncur (▷ 89)
Cafe Sydney (▷ 51)
Cruise Bar (▷ 51)
Dolphin Hotel (▷ 89)
Dunbar House (▷ 106)
Est (▷ 51)
MCA Café (▷ 51)
Momofuku Seiobo (▷ 66)
The Pavilion (▷ 90)
Pony Dining (▷ 52)
Q Dining (▷ 52)
Quarryman's Hotel (▷ 66)

Cafés
Bills (▷ 89)
Fine Food Store (▷ 51)

Chinese
BBQ King (▷ 66)
Eating World (▷ 66)
Fisherman's Wharf (▷ 66)
The Malaya (▷ 66)
Mr Wong (▷ 51)
Neptune Palace (▷ 51)

Indian
Flavour of India (▷ 89)

Italian
Bondi Trattoria (▷ 106)
Iceberg's Dining Room (▷ 106)
Lucio's (▷ 90)

Japanese
Ippudo (▷ 90)
Saké (▷ 52)
Tetsuya's (▷ 90)

Mexican
Mejico (▷ 66)

Modern Med
Bathers Pavilion (▷ 36)

Other European
Bodega (▷ 89)
Continental Deli Bar Bistro (▷ 106)
Quay Bar (▷ 52)
Sir Stamford at Circular Quay (▷ 52)

Seafood
Balkan Seafood (▷ 89)
Catalina (▷ 106)
Doyles on the Beach (▷ 106)
Quay (▷ 52)
Rockpool Bar & Grill (▷ 52)
Sydney Cove Oyster Bar (▷ 36)

Thai
Bo Thai (▷ 36)
Longrain (▷ 90)
Spice I Am (▷ 90)
Wild Ginger Dining + Bar (▷ 52)

Vietnamese
Red Lantern (▷ 90)

Top Tips For...

These great suggestions will help you tailor your ideal visit to Sydney, no matter how you choose to spend your time. Each sight or listing has a fuller write-up elsewhere in the book.

SAMPLING LOCAL CUISINE
Sample the Chinese cuisine at Mr Wong (▷ 51), a Sydneysider favorite for its Cantonese food and colonial decor.
Sydney's best seafood cuisine can be enjoyed at Rockpool Bar & Grill (▷ 52), set in a stylish art deco building on Hunter Street.

OUTDOOR DINING
Boasting stunning ocean vistas, Icebergs Dining Room (▷ 106) at Bondi serves tasty Mediterranean fare in a great setting.
Sit outdoors at Sydney's most famous seafood restaurant, Doyles on the Beach (▷ 106) at Watsons Bay and enjoy waterside views with the CBD in the distance.

BUDGET CLOTHING
Paddy's Markets (▷ 63) sells quality brand clothing as well as men's and women's underwear and lingerie.
Head for Paddington Markets (▷ 86) in Oxford Street on Saturday, for original designs, alternative fashions and casual wear.

FREE THINGS
At the Royal Botanic Garden Sydney (▷ 24–25) you can stroll among a great plant collection in a superb setting.
See some of Australia's most admired paintings, sculptures and decorative arts at the Art Gallery of New South Wales (▷ 70–71).
At the Rocks Discovery Museum you can learn about the fascinating history of The Rocks (▷ 43).
Head to The Domain (▷ 24) for guided walks during the day, and concerts, including opera, under the stars.

Clockwise from top left: pretty as a picture—seafood on a plate; kids' delight; having fun in the city; take a break at

LEARNING ABOUT LOCAL CULTURE

An excellent collection of decorative arts, including many utilitarian objects from the past, can be viewed at the Powerhouse Museum (▷ 59) at Pyrmont.

The Australian Museum (▷ 72–73) has one of the world's best collections of Aboriginal cultural objects in its permanent exhibition.

GOING OUT ON THE TOWN

Dress up and make your way to Blu Bar on 36 (▷ 50) where the cocktails are served with a stunning Harbour backdrop.

If you feel like a flutter, The Star (▷ 62) offers slot machines, blackjack, roulette and a host of other games of chance, but remember to dress up smart.

STAYING AT BUDGET HOTELS

At the centrally located Song Hotel (▷ 109) there are stylish rooms (some themed to celebrate prominent Australian women) with the option of en-suite or shared bathrooms.

In a quiet street close to the action, the Metro Aspire (▷ 109) has refurbished rooms with balconies and bathrooms. Book direct for deals like breakfast for a dollar!

ENTERTAINING THE KIDS

At City Farm (▷ 105) adults can have as much fun as kids interacting with the many farm animals on display.

The Powerhouse Museum (▷ 59) has lots of things to see and hands-on exhibits that keep young ones—and some of the old ones, too—entertained.

At Wild Life Sydney Zoo (▷ 62) kids can meet Australian animals, enjoy ranger talks and even get to feed some of the residents.

Have fun at Luna Park (▷ 34), a historic, colorful amusement park that's free to enter (but you need a ticket to ride).

Go on an Art Safari at the MCA (▷ 40), which runs a range of family-friendly art programs for kids.

Bondi; Angora lambs down at the farm; soak up some culture at the Art Gallery of NSW; alfresco dining

A GIRLS' NIGHT OUT

One of Sydney's most popular pubs, the Mercantile Hotel (▷ 50) at The Rocks, has live music most nights.

At Cherry (▷ 64), at The Star in Pyrmont, you can sip cocktails and hear house, disco and Balearic beat.

A WALK ON THE WILD SIDE

Sydney Harbour National Park (▷ 28–29) has lots of walking trails where you can discover original native vegetation.

The scenic Blue Mountains (▷ 102), just over an hour's drive from the CBD, has many forest walking trails. Its towns boast excellent hotels, restaurants and quaint shops.

CUTTING-EDGE ARCHITECTURE

One of the world's most dramatic buildings, the Sydney Opera House (▷ 30–31) has a tour that reveals its design history.

Chifley Tower (▷ 79) has a unique shape and an excellent shopping mall that includes a food court.

On a smaller, more domestic scale, the 1950s Rose Seidler House (▷ 101) remains one of the most iconic examples of mid-century architecture in Australia.

BIRDS, BEASTS AND ANIMALS

Check out one of Australia's top wildlife parks, Koala Park Sanctuary (▷ 100), set in the forest at West Pennant Hills.

Home to the full range of Australia's wildlife—including platypus, echidna, kangaroo and koala—Taronga Zoo (▷ 32–33) also has a dramatic setting on the water's edge.

For fans of slithering creatures, the Australian Reptile Park (▷ 105) has a beautiful bush setting and an array of impressive reptiles, as well as native animals, spiders and amphibians.

Go whale-watching in the Harbour on a whale-watching cruise (▷ 36). There are various cruises operating throughout the day right up until sunset.

Have a night on the tiles or take a trip to the country; Sydney Opera House; spot the joey in the koala's pouch

Sydney by Area

and North Sydney

The magnificent and iconic Harbour, around which Sydney has developed, is both a transport route and a recreational domain from where you'll see the city at its finest.

Top 25

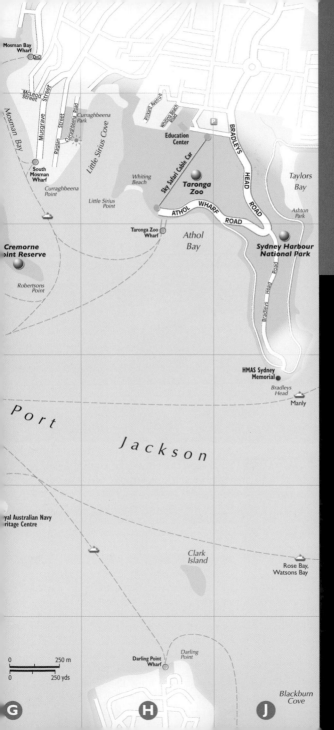

Mosman Bay
Wharf

McLeod
Street

Mosman Bay

Musgrave Street

Raglan Street

Curraghbeena Road

Curraghbeena Park

Little Sirius Cove

Prichard Avenue

Whiting Beach Road

Education Center

Sky Safari Cable Car

Taronga Zoo

P

BRADLEYS HEAD ROAD

Taylors Bay

South Mosman Wharf

Curraghbeena Point

Whiting Beach

Little Sirius Point

ATHOL WHARF ROAD

Ashton Park

Taronga Zoo Wharf

Athol Bay

Sydney Harbour National Park

Cremorne Point Reserve

Robertsons Point

Bradleys Head Road

HMAS Sydney Memorial

Bradleys Head

Manly

P o r t

J a c k s o n

yal Australian Navy
eritage Centre

Clark Island

Rose Bay, Watsons Bay

0   250 m

0   250 yds

Darling Point Wharf

Darling Point

Blackburn Cove

G   **H**   **J**

Sydney Harbour and North Sydney

Royal Botanic Garden Sydney and the Domain

HIGHLIGHTS

- Sydney Tropical Centre
- Sydney Fernery
- Palm Grove
- Herb Garden
- Visitor Centre
- Gardens Shop
- Free guided walks
- Government House
- Walk around Farm Cove to Mrs Macquaries Point
- Views from Mrs Macquaries Point
- Scenic train tour by Choo-Choo Express
- The Calyx

To escape the crowds of central Sydney, visit the glorious Botanic Garden, once an Aboriginal sacred site, then take a stroll in the Domain, a waterside haven for kookaburras and cockatoos.

Royal Botanic Garden Sydney Founded in 1816, these magnificent gardens now contain a finely curated collection of native and foreign plants (and native critters). Don't miss the contemporary glasshouses containing the Sydney Fernery and the Sydney Tropical Centre. High-speed WiFi means you can learn about the plants via an app as you wander around the greenery. You can take a tour, learn about Aboriginal culture, stop in at the gorgeous garden shop and even chill out with a yoga class in The Calyx, a stunning exhibition space built in

From far left: the main pond at the Royal Botanic Garden Sydney; plants with Bite exhibition; the Spring Walk features a mix of flowers, shrubs and trees

the heart of the garden in 2016. Government House, once the official residence of the governor of New South Wales, lies within the garden too, and tours are open to the public.

The Domain The northern section of the Domain (the remainder fronts the Art Gallery of NSW on the other side of the Cahill Expressway and is used mainly by lunchtime joggers and for open-air concerts in summer) is part of the land laid out in 1810 as the "domain" of Governor Macquarie. This tree-lined area is a lovely spot for picnics and waterfront strolls. In summer, you can have a dip at the open-air Andrew "Boy" Charlton swimming pool and walk to Mrs Macquaries Point, named after the governor's wife who, not surprisingly, enjoyed the wonderful view from this promontory.

THE BASICS

rbgsyd.nsw.gov.au

✚ E6

✉ Mrs Macquaries Road

☎ Botanic Garden 9231 8111; Government House infoline 9228 4111

🕐 Garden: daily from 7am. Closing is seasonal and varies from 5–7.30pm. The Calyx: daily 10–4

🍴 Botanic Garden Restaurant: daily 12–3; weekend breakfast 9.30–11.30. Pavilion Restaurant: daily breakfast from 9am, lunch 12–3

🚉 Circular Quay/Martin Place, St. James

🚌 200, 441

🚢 Circular Quay

♿ Very good

🎟 Free

Sydney Harbour

TOP 25

A striking contrast of views over Sydney Harbour

THE BASICS

sydney.com.au
🔢 E4
✉ Fort Denison, Sydney Harbour
☎ 1800 067 676
🕐 Tours daily of Circular Quay and The Rocks
🚉 Circular Quay
🚌 Free shuttle or all buses bound for Circular Quay
🚢 From Circular Quay

HIGHLIGHTS

● Ferry ride or cruise
● Fort Denison
● Views from South Head and North Head
● Goat Island
● The Spit to Manly Walk (▷ 101)
● Picnic on Shark Island

TIP

● Choose your day carefully for a boat trip if you are prone to sea sickness.

Spectacular Sydney Harbour, officially Port Jackson, undoubtedly makes this city special. You get stunning water views from the most unexpected places and the still waters are a wonderful place for sailing. Be sure to take a ferry ride to Manly.

Sydney Harbour With a shoreline that stretches 240km (149 miles), Sydney Harbour is guaranteed to delight. The best way to enjoy this setting is to take a ferry ride or cruise, most of which depart from Circular Quay—you can even travel on an elegant square-rigged schooner. You can visit beautiful Cremorne Point, Taronga Zoo (▷ 32–33), Manly (▷ 95) and Watsons Bay (▷ 101), or take an evening cruise to view the city lights. Harborside walks, such as those around North Head or South Head, are popular, while Sydney Harbour National Park (▷ 28–29) encompasses Shark, Clark, Goat and Rodd islands. After you have taken in the obvious attractions of the main part of the Harbour, head west beyond the Harbour Bridge or take a RiverCat trip upriver to Parramatta or Homebush Bay, or travel by ferry to the suburbs of Balmain, Birchgrove, Greenwich, Hunters Hill and Meadowbank.

Fort Denison This island was once known as "Pinchgut", after the practice of marooning disobedient convicts here with very meager rations. By 1857 the island had become Fort Denison, built to defend Sydney against possible Russian invasion during the Crimean War.

Sydney Harbour Bridge

An iconic view of Sydney Harbour Bridge and the Opera House in the late evening

Affectionately called "the coat hanger" by locals, the Sydney Harbour Bridge is one of the most famous symbols of this city. Take a climb to the top of the bridge for great views, an energetic climb that's not for the fainthearted.

All things to all people This bridge is an essential link between the south and north sides of the Harbour, the perfect backdrop to the Opera House, and a great spot to take in the panorama. The world's widest long-span bridge was opened in March 1932. The arch spans 503m (1,650ft) and the bridge carries eight road lanes, two railway tracks, a cycleway and footpath. Crossing by car, bus or train just isn't the same—the best experience is walking across. From the city side, access to the walkway is via Argyle Street in The Rocks, while the northern entrance is near Milsons Point station; a ferry service operates between Milsons Point and Circular Quay.

Take in the view The highlight of a walk across the bridge is a stop at the southeast pylon. There is an interesting display here on how the bridge was constructed, and the 200-step climb to the lookout is well worthwhile for the magnificent views of the Harbour and the city.

BridgeClimb For a bird's-eye view of the city and surrounds take the three-hour climb to the top of the bridge's arch with a professional guide; strict safety measures are in place.

THE BASICS

sydney.com.au/bridge.html
🔁 D4
☎ 9240 1100; pylonlookout.com.au
☎ 8274 7777; bridgeclimb.com
🕐 Lookout: daily 10–5
🚉 Circular Quay (southern side)
🚌 Sydney Explorer
🚉 Milsons Point (northern side)
⛴ Circular Quay (southern side)
♿ Walkway free. Pylon Lookout: moderate. BridgeClimb: expensive

HIGHLIGHTS

● The walk across
● View from the Pylon Lookout
● Pylon Lookout display
● Close-up look at the structure
● A climb to the top of the bridge
● New Year's Eve fireworks

Sydney Harbour National Park

HIGHLIGHTS

- Fort Denison
- Shark Island
- Quarantine Station
- Nielsen Park
- Middle Head forts

TIPS

- Be sure to pack a hat, sunscreen and protective clothing for the ferry journeys.
- Drones are not permitted in the park.

There is no better way to get to know the many stunning bays and inlets and their surrounding suburbs than by exploring the multisectioned Sydney Harbour National Park.

Early days The park contains remnants of the bushland that was common before white settlement, and many heritage attractions. You can visit convict-built buildings, historic maritime and military installations and recreational islands. The Quarantine Station (▷ 100) at North Head, which isolated new arrivals with infectious diseases from Sydneysiders, has nighttime ghost walks. At Middle Head are the remains of forts built around the Harbour for protection from, among others, Russians in the 19th century and the Japanese in the 1940s.

Clockwise from far left: a view across the water from Bradleys Head; stained-glass window at Watson's Chapel at South Head in the National Park; plenty of space in the park; Sydney skyline with Clark Island in the mid-distance; kookaburra in the park; a view of Sydney Harbour

Other park highlights Ferry tours visit the tiny colonial penal relic of Fort Denison, Australia's only Martello tower. Here an audiovisual presentation highlights its history, including its time as a high-security prison. Enjoy a relaxing ferry trip to tiny Shark Island, set in the middle of Sydney Harbour. With its trees and picnic shelters, this is perfect for a picnic—there is even a small beach where you can enjoy a swim. There are many walks, such as the Manly Scenic Walkway, with its native coastal heath and pockets of subtropical rainforest. On the south side of the Harbour, the 1.5km (1-mile), Hermitage Foreshore Track starts in Nielsen Park at Vaucluse and leads through a strip of protected bushland, winding along the western edge of Vaucluse and finishing at Bayview Hill Road. A swim at Nielsen Park beach is a treat.

THE BASICS

nationalparks.nsw. gov.au

➕ J3

✉ Information: Cadman's Cottage, George Street, The Rocks

☎ 1300 072 757

🚢 Fort Denison tours run daily from Circular Quay. Shark Island ferries run from Darling Harbour and Circular Quay

✋ Moderate

Sydney Opera House

This once controversial, yet ethereal, sail-roofed building rising from the water on its prominent bayside site epitomizes the free-spirited nature of this young and vibrant city.

Sydney's most recognizable building The Opera House was conceived by Danish architect Jørn Utzon, who won a design competition in 1959. It took 14 years to create this masterpiece, which was opened in October 1973 by Queen Elizabeth II, and the project was fraught with technical and political problems (Utzon eventually resigned). The building holds six performance halls—for plays, dance, symphony concerts, opera and other events—restaurants and bars, and a maze of backstage areas. The open-air forecourt turns the Harbour into a

Clockwise from far left: people abseiling on the roof of Sydney Opera House; interior of the magnificent concert hall; take a ferry past the famous building; crowds come out to view the Harbour on Australia Day

stage. The roofs are covered with more than a million ceramic tiles, and the stone base and terraces are fashioned on the Mayan and Aztec temples of Mexico. You can enjoy the exterior at any time; a walk around is an excellent way to enjoy the views.

The interior While the architect's vision for the interior was never fully realized, there is much to see here including a John Olsen mural, *Salute to Five Bells*, in the northern foyer of the Concert Hall, and a Michael Tjakamarra mural, titled *Possum Dreaming*, in the foyer of the Opera Theatre. Take a walk around the building for a different perspective of the CBD and the Harbour Bridge. If possible, attend a performance or take a guided tour to fully appreciate this world-famous icon.

THE BASICS

sydneyoperahouse.
com
➕ E4
✉ Bennelong Point
☎ Tours and box office: 9250 7777
🕐 Tours daily 7–5. Performances most days.
🍴 Four restaurants and cafés also theater bars
🚆 Circular Quay
🚌 Any Circular Quay bus
⛴ Circular Quay
♿ Good
👝 Tours: expensive

Taronga Zoo

Residents at Sydney's Taronga Zoo

THE BASICS

taronga.org.au
H2
Bradleys Head Road, Mosman
9969 2777
Daily 9.30–5
The View restaurant, Taronga Food Market and picnic areas
M30, 238
Taronga Zoo
Good
Expensive

HIGHLIGHTS

- Western Lowland gorillas
- Australian Walkabout
- Snow leopards
- Seal shows
- "Orang-utan Walk"
- White Sumatran tiger
- Platypus and echidna
- Views from the cable car
- Koalas
- Rainforest Aviary

TIP

- Arrive by ferry and take the Sky Safari up to the top.

Located in Sydney Harbour, Taronga Zoo is a conservation leader. Although it doesn't limit itself to native animals, its Australian animals are most popular. The ferry ride to get there is a bonus.

Australian wildlife Set in natural foreshore bushland, Taronga (an Aboriginal word meaning water view) dates from 1916 and has long been at the forefront of animal care and conservation. Home to 4,000 animals, many from threatened species, this is a picturesque place to get up close to Australia's famed native fauna, including koalas, kangaroos, quokkas, echidnas and all manner of spectacular birds. There are also high rope courses, where you can get memorable views of the Harbour while you swing high above the Zoo, as well as talks, tours and the chance to have an up-close encounter with your favorite resident. For the ultimate immersive experience, stay overnight on a Roar and Snore package.

Creatures from other countries Taronga's strong support for wildlife conservation is evident in its endangered species breeding agenda; the zoo is home to Sumatran tigers (book a spot on the Tiger Trek, an Indonesian-themed immersive and educational experience that takes you up-close to these incredible animals), Himalayan snow leopards, red pandas, Western Lowland gorillas, black rhinoceros, Asian elephants, chimpanzees and Fijian crested iguanas.

More to See

CREMORNE POINT RESERVE

northsydney.nsw.gov.au

A walk at this reserve reveals a part of the city visitors seldom see. From the wharf, turn left and walk along the reserve's western section, which gives fine views of the city. Walk up the steps opposite the wharf and head left, where you can stroll around the waterside, past gardens and homes with outlooks to tranquil Mosman Bay. From here, the ferry will take you to Circular Quay.

G3 ⊠ Cremorne ☎ 9936 8100 ⏰ Daily 🚶 Free

LUNA PARK

lunaparksydney.com

This restored 1930s amusement park, set on the Harbour foreshores, has crazy rides including a roller coaster, games and attractions for kids during school holidays.

D3 ⊠ 1 Olympic Drive, Milsons Point ☎ 9922 6644 ⏰ Daily hours vary; check website for operational rides 🍴 Bar and food outlets 🚆 Milsons Point 🚢 Milsons Point 🚶 Expensive

MARY MACKILLOP MUSEUM

marymackillopplace.org.au

Beatified in 1995, Mary MacKillop championed the poor in Australia. State-of-the-art electronics, theatrics and animatronics show Mary's life.

Off map at C1 ⊠ Mary MacKillop Place, 7 Mount Street, North Sydney ☎ 8912 4878 ⏰ Daily 10–4 🍴 Coffee shop 🚆 North Sydney 🚶 Moderate

NORTH SYDNEY

taronga.org.au

The suburb of North Sydney has a collection of office buildings and retail outlets that border the Harbour.

D2 ⊠ North Sydney 🍴 Many cafés and restaurants 🚆 North Sydney (from CBD) 🚌 261, 263

SYDNEY HARBOUR CRUISES

sydneyharbourcruises.com.au

Learn about the Harbour, its bays and waterways on a variety of cruises.

F4 ⊠ Captain Cook Cruises, No. 6 Jetty, Circular Quay ☎ 9206 1122 ⏰ Daily from 9.30am 🍴 Coffee and dinner cruises 🚆 Circular Quay 🚶 Moderate

Discover the latest rides and attractions at Luna Park

Taronga Zoo to
Balmoral Beach

This interesting Harbour walk runs along the northern foreshores and features spectacular views, historic sights and natural bushland.

DISTANCE: 6km (4 miles) **ALLOW**: 3 hours

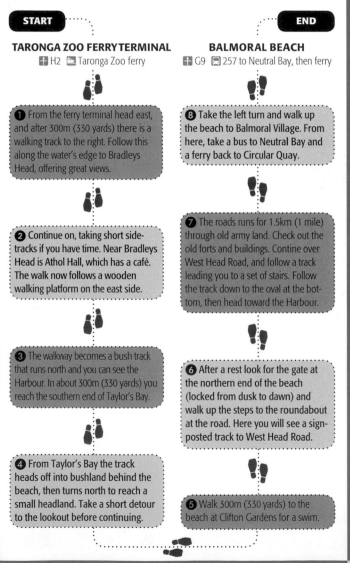

START · · · · · ·

END

TARONGA ZOO FERRY TERMINAL
🚏 H2 ⛴ Taronga Zoo ferry

BALMORAL BEACH
🚏 G9 🚌 257 to Neutral Bay, then ferry

1 From the ferry terminal head east, and after 300m (330 yards) there is a walking track to the right. Follow this along the water's edge to Bradleys Head, offering great views.

8 Take the left turn and walk up the beach to Balmoral Village. From here, take a bus to Neutral Bay and a ferry back to Circular Quay.

2 Continue on, taking short side-tracks if you have time. Near Bradleys Head is Athol Hall, which has a café. The walk now follows a wooden walking platform on the east side.

7 The roads runs for 1.5km (1 mile) through old army land. Check out the old forts and buildings. Contine over West Head Road, and follow a track leading you to a set of stairs. Follow the track down to the oval at the bottom, then head toward the Harbour.

3 The walkway becomes a bush track that runs north and you can see the Harbour. In about 300m (330 yards) you reach the southern end of Taylor's Bay.

6 After a rest look for the gate at the northern end of the beach (locked from dusk to dawn) and walk up the steps to the roundabout at the road. Here you will see a sign-posted track to West Head Road.

4 From Taylor's Bay the track heads off into bushland behind the beach, then turns north to reach a small headland. Take a short detour to the lookout before continuing.

5 Walk 300m (330 yards) to the beach at Clifton Gardens for a swim.

Entertainment and Nightlife

NORTH SYDNEY OLYMPIC POOL

This harborside pool is open-air in summer, but covered by a "bubble" in cooler months. Spa and sauna upstairs.

🔢 D3 ✉ 4 Alfred Street South, Milsons Point ☎ 9955 2309 🕐 Mon–Fri 5.30am–9pm, Sat–Sun 7–7 🚉 Milsons Point

OZ JET BOATING

ozjetboating.com

Explore Sydney Harbour at speed by a thrilling jet boat ride.

🔢 D5 ✉ Circular Quay's Eastern Pontoon ☎ 9808 3700 🕐 Daily summer 11–5, winter 11–4 🚉 Circular Quay ⛴ Circular Quay

WHALE WATCHING

sydneywhalewatching.com

Commentaries on whales and Harbour sights. Departures from Darling Harbour, Circular Quay and Manly.

🔢 C6 ✉ Wharf 6/Pier 26/Aquarium Wharf ☎ 9583 1199 🕐 Mid-May to early Dec, 2- and 3-hour cruises 🚉 Town Hall

Where to Eat

Prices are approximate, based on a 3-course meal for one person.

$$$	over A$60
$$	A$40–A$60
$	under A$40

BATHERS' PAVILION ($$$)

batherspavilion.com.au

Lush interior with views over the beach. Offers modern European-style, particularly French, dishes with the emphasis on fresh produce. There's a more casual café, too.

🔢 J2 ✉ 4 The Esplanade, Mosman ☎ 9969 5050 🕐 Daily lunch, dinner

BO THAI ($$)

bothai.com.au

The cream-colored decor and greenery are soothing and there's a menu of Thai classics with deft little twists, like lamb cutlets with a Thai-spiced crumb or tiger prawns with salmon roe.

🔢 E2 ✉ 16 Willoughby Road, Crows Nest ☎ 9966 9831 🕐 Daily lunch, dinner 🚉 C343

SYDNEY COVE OYSTER BAR ($$–$$$)

sydneycoveoysterbar.com

Here you'll find light and tasty seafood in a stunning Harbour setting near the Opera House. Enjoy panoramic waterside views from the outdoor seating.

🔢 E5 ✉ 1 Circular Quay East ☎ 9247 2937 🕐 Daily snacks, lunch, dinner 🚉 Circular Quay

FOOD AFLOAT

There is no better way to experience the Harbour's magic than by dining on the water. Although the cuisine of these floating restaurants rarely reaches gourmet standards, lunch or dinner cruises are popular. Operators include Captain Cook Cruises (☎ 9206 1111), Matilda Cruises (☎ 8270 5188) and Clearview Sydney Harbour Glass Boat Dinner Cruises (☎ 8296 7353) for the ultimate view.

Circular Quay and The Rocks

This waterside precinct, the historic core of Sydney, has fine views of the Harbour Bridge and Opera House, and is accessible on foot. The Rocks has some of the best restored buildings in the city.

3 Drummoyne, Woolwich

Goat Island

Walsh Bay

Dawes Point
Pier One

DAWES POINT

Millers Point

Wharf Theatre

Barangaroo Reserve

4

Towns Place

Dalgety Road

Hickson Road

Potlinger Street

Fort Street

Hickson Road

HICKSON HIGHWAY A4

THE ROCKS

Windmill Street

Merriman Street

MILLERS POINT

Argyle Place

Lower Fort Street

Argyle Street

BRADFIELD

Playfair St

Sydney Observatory

Kent Street

Hickson Road

Upper Fort Street

Gloucester St

Cumberland

Mill Gates

i

Museum of Contemporary

Susannah Place Museum

5

Johnstons Bay

BARANGAROO

Watermans Quai

P

Maritime Centre

P

Cumberland St

Gloucester St

Harrington

St

George

Street

St

CAHILL EXPRESSWAY

Alfre

Pier Street

P

Grosvenor Place

GROSVENOR STREET

Dalley Street

Bridg

WESTERN DISTRIBUTOR

P **P**

P

6

7

0 ——————— 250 m
0 ——————— 250 yds

B   **C**   **D**

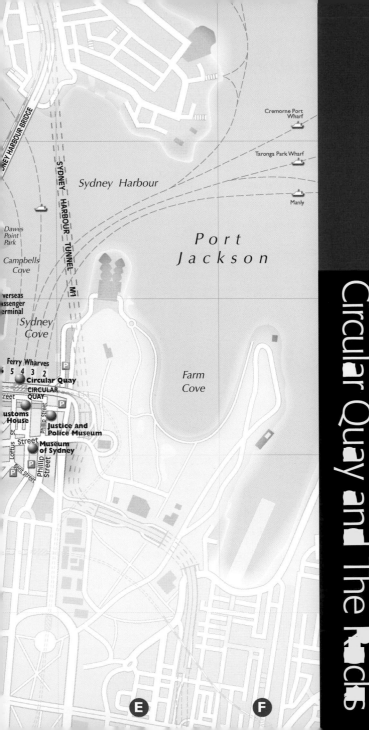

SYDNEY HARBOUR BRIDGE

SYDNEY HARBOUR TUNNEL

M1

Sydney Harbour

Cremorne Port Wharf

Taronga Park Wharf

Manly

Port Jackson

Dawes Point Park

Campbells Cove

verseas assenger erminal

Sydney Cove

Ferry Wharves

5 4 3 2 **Circular Quay**

CIRCULAR QUAY

reet

ustoms House

Loftus St

Street

Phillip Street

Justice and Police Museum

Museum of Sydney

Phillip Street

Bent Street

Farm Cove

E

F

Museum of Contemporary Art

- Art deco building
- Visiting exhibitions
- Indigenous art
- Free guided tours
- MCA shop and café

TIP

- Wheelchairs can be borrowed from the information desk at no charge.

The MCA is a modern art gallery full of surprises. Stunning installations, audacious photography, fine Aboriginal art and special performances all combine to astound and entertain.

The museum In a superb location overlooking the Harbour, the MCA contains Australia's finest collection of contemporary art. Established in 1991 by the University of Sydney, through a bequest of John Wardell Power and the provision of the building by the state government, the MCA contains more than 4,000 works. International visiting exhibitions, ranging from photography to 3D installations, are a highlight and often occupy a large part of the gallery space, sending much of the permanent collection into temporary storage.

Clockwise from far left: photographic display at the Museum of Contemporary Art; puppy installation by Jeff Koons seen outside the museum during the Festival of Sydney; the museum's attractive waterside location; displays of modern art and installations

The permanent collection The Australian and international art exhibits date from the 1960s and include indigenous art from the Northern Territory's Arnhem Land, the Contemporary Art Archive and work by overseas artists such as Andy Warhol and Roy Lichtenstein.

The building This old building was once home to the Maritime Services Board. The structure was designed in 1939 but was not completed until 1954 due to the shortages of building materials and labor during the war. This makes it the last art deco style building in Sydney. Both the MCA Restaurant and the MCA Café offer magnificent views of the Opera House, and you'll find jewelry, bags, greeting cards, and an excellent range of books covering all aspects of contemporary art in the MCA Store.

THE BASICS

mca.com.au

✚ D5

✉ 140 George Street, The Rocks

☎ 9245 2458

🕐 Daily 10–5, Wed 10–9

🍴 Restaurant, café

🚇 Circular Quay

🚌 431

⛴ Circular Quay

♿ Excellent

✋ Free

❓ There are numerous free tours of both the permanent and special collections. Check online for the schedule

Museum of Sydney

The slick, modern building houses a treasure trove of the city's historic objects

TOP 25

THE BASICS

sydneylivingmuseums.
com.au

🔢 D5

✉ Corner of Bridge and Phillip streets

☎ 9251 5988

🕙 Daily 10–5

🍴 Restaurant

🚆 Circular Quay

🚌 Any Circular Quay-bound bus

⛴ Circular Quay

♿ Excellent

✋ Moderate

HIGHLIGHTS

● *Edge of the Trees* sculpture and the public square
● Original Government House foundations
● Video wall
● State-of-the-art installations
● First Fleet model ships
● Changing exhibitions

This unusual museum leads you on a journey of discovery from the local Aboriginal occupation and the convict days of the late 18th century to the Sydney of the 1850s and beyond.

The site The location forms an integral part of this exciting museum, for it was here that the nation's first, modest Government House was built in 1788. Home to the first nine governors, the building was demolished in 1846, but excavations have revealed the original foundations, part of which can be viewed through the paving. Emphasizing the nation's mixed origins, the dramatic forecourt sculpture, *Edge of the Trees*, consisting of 29 massive pillars of sandstone, wood and steel, symbolizes the first Aboriginal encounter with the invading Europeans.

The museum Divided into several themed areas and laid out in an imaginative minimalist style, the Museum of Sydney aims to interpret the city's past, present and future. Stories of the indigenous Gadigal people and the early European days are told through objects found during excavations, computer displays, a 33-screen video wall and spoken history.

Gadigal Place Gallery The exhibition in this one-room gallery tells the stories of individual indigenous Australians who had contact with early settlers. Traditional cultural items are on display and you can watch a video of Aboriginal people talking about their lives and memories.

THE BASICS

therocks.com

🕂 D5

✉ Sydney Visitor Centre, The Rocks, corner of Argyle and Playfair streets

☎ 8273 0000 or 1800 067 676

🕐 Daily 9.30–5.30.

🍴 Many cafés and restaurants nearby

🚉 Circular Quay

🚌 431, 433

🚢 Circular Quay

♿ Generally good

🎫 Free

The district known as The Rocks, Sydney's first "village", has a fascinating history as a colonial port area. Many of the restored old buildings now house interesting shops, restaurants and pubs.

A rocky start Named after the shore where convict tents were erected in January 1788, The Rocks is Sydney's most intriguing and picturesque area. It was once the province of seamen and traders, thieves and prostitutes, and the scene of a 1900 outbreak of bubonic plague that claimed more than 100 lives. During the 1920s, entire streets were demolished to make way for the southern approach to the Harbour Bridge, but detailed restoration since 1970 has transformed the district into a tourist hub. The area is packed with attractions, and these will easily fill a day—there are many 1900s buildings to admire, narrow streets such as Nurses Walk and Suez Canal to explore, and lots of shops and cafés. Campbells Cove, with its historic warehouses next to the Harbour Bridge, and Dawes Point Park under the bridge are both popular waterfront spots. The Rocks also offers many museums and galleries that are well worth visiting.

Sydney Visitor Centre, The Rocks The best place to start is at the Visitor Centre. This tour-booking and information outlet contains a shop and a display that covers the history of The Rocks. You can also reserve accommodations and activities, and find out what's on.

HIGHLIGHTS

● Campbells Cove
● Suez Canal and Nurses Walk
● The Rocks Market on weekends (▷ 50)
● Views from Dawes Point Park
● Local museums

TIP

● Take The Rocks walking tour, starting at Shop 4A, Clocktower Square, on the corner of Argyle and Harrington streets.

Sydney Observatory

Sydney's glittering night skies are as intriguing today as they were for Australia's early astronomers, who built this fine building high on Observatory Hill in 1858.

The Observatory and Observatory Hill The Observatory, now a museum of astronomy and related sciences, provides a glimpse into those subjects through hands-on exhibits and other displays. This is also the location for one of Sydney's most unusual activities—night-sky viewing (reserved in advance). Observatory Hill is the city's highest point (44m/119ft) and was the site of Fort Phillip (1803), the original 1821 Observatory and the Signal Station (1848), which still stands. There are great inner-Harbour views from the hill and you can walk behind the

Observatory to visit the National Trust Centre, with its S. H. Ervin Gallery and excellent tea-rooms. The gallery features changing exhibitions of Australian art and culture, ranging from watercolor paintings to photography.

Argyle Place Just below Observatory Hill, and flanked by historic houses and the 1840 Gothic-revival Garrison Church, is Argyle Place. Also here is the Lord Nelson Hotel (1834). A stroll down nearby Lower Fort Street reveals more 19th-century terraced (row) houses and the oddly shaped Hero of Waterloo Hotel (1843), named for the Duke of Wellington, best known for defeating Napoleon at the Battle of Waterloo. From just above Argyle Place, you can walk, via the covered steps, on to the Sydney Harbour Bridge walkway.

THE BASICS

maas.museum/sydney-observatory

➕ C5

✉ Watson Road, Observatory Hill, Millers Point

☎ 9217 0111

🕐 Daily 10–5 (late opening evenings according to season, check website for details)

🍴 Café nearby

🚆 Circular Quay

🚌 431

⛴ Circular Quay

♿ Few

✋ Free; charge for night viewing (moderate)

☎ 9921 3485

More to See

CIRCULAR QUAY

sydney.com.au/quay.htm

The focal point of Sydney's maritime life since European settlement, Circular Quay is today a bustling pedestrian precinct with ferry, bus and rail terminals, as well as busy cafés—the perfect spot for a coffee. Be sure to check out the galleries, library and restaurants in nearby Customs House. The covered walkway from the Opera House includes Writers Walk, with plaques commemorating some prominent Australian authors, poets and playwrights. The surrounding precinct of Circular Quay West contains Cadman's Cottage, the city's oldest building (1816). It is now a national parks and wildlife information area (☎ 9253 0888). Also in this area is First Fleet Park, commemorating the nation's first settlers, and the large Overseas Passenger Terminal, with viewing platforms and dining.

➕ D5 ✉ Circular Quay 🍴 Cafés and restaurants 🚇 Circular Quay 🚌 Various 🎟 Moderate

CUSTOMS HOUSE

sydneycustomshouse.com.au

From 1845 to 1990 this was home to the Customs Service, but today the building's interior is a major cultural venue. There are galleries, a public library and reading room, cafés, studios and a performance space. The lounge area has WiFi, work stations and magazines.

➕ D5 ✉ 31 Alfred Street ☎ 9242 8551 🕐 Mon–Fri 8am midnight, Sat 10am–midnight, Sun 11–5 🍴 Cafés 🚇 Circular Quay 🎟 Free

JUSTICE AND POLICE MUSEUM

sydneylivingmuseums.com.au

Originally the Water Police Court (1856), these old buildings now house a museum of legal and police history. The complex includes the Magistrate's Court, exhibitions in the cells and a museum of crime, the latter featuring mug shots of some of early Sydney's criminals.

➕ D5 ✉ Corner Albert and Phillip streets ☎ 9252 1144 🕐 Sat–Sun 10–5 🍴 Nearby 🚇 Circular Quay 🎟 Moderate

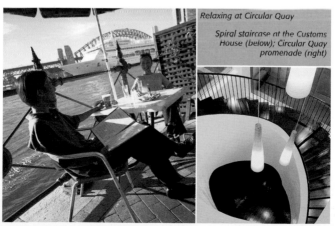

Relaxing at Circular Quay

Spiral staircase at the Customs House (below); Circular Quay promenade (right)

Circular Quay to the Art Gallery

Tour the Harbour's edge to see the Opera House, then the Art Gallery of NSW, via a walk through the Royal Botanic Garden Sydney.

DISTANCE: 4km (2.5 miles) **ALLOW:** 2 hours (plus visits to Opera House and Gallery)

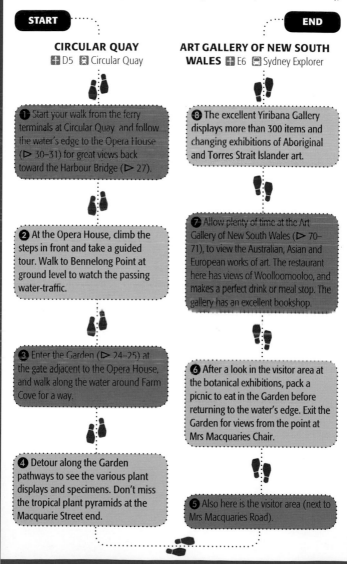

START

CIRCULAR QUAY
⊞ D5 🚇 Circular Quay

END

ART GALLERY OF NEW SOUTH WALES ⊞ E6 🚌 Sydney Explorer

❶ Start your walk from the ferry terminals at Circular Quay and follow the water's edge to the Opera House (▷ 30–31) for great views back toward the Harbour Bridge (▷ 27).

❽ The excellent Yiribana Gallery displays more than 300 items and changing exhibitions of Aboriginal and Torres Strait Islander art.

❷ At the Opera House, climb the steps in front and take a guided tour. Walk to Bennelong Point at ground level to watch the passing water-traffic.

❼ Allow plenty of time at the Art Gallery of New South Wales (▷ 70–71), to view the Australian, Asian and European works of art. The restaurant here has views of Woolloomooloo, and makes a perfect drink or meal stop. The gallery has an excellent bookshop.

❸ Enter the Garden (▷ 24–25) at the gate adjacent to the Opera House, and walk along the water around Farm Cove for a way.

❻ After a look in the visitor area at the botanical exhibitions, pack a picnic to eat in the Garden before returning to the water's edge. Exit the Garden for views from the point at Mrs Macquaries Chair.

❹ Detour along the Garden pathways to see the various plant displays and specimens. Don't miss the tropical plant pyramids at the Macquarie Street end.

❺ Also here is the visitor area (next to Mrs Macquaries Road).

Shopping

ABORIGINAL ART GALLERIES

aboriginalartgalleries.com.au

Displays authentic artworks, craft, ceramics, glass and didgeridoos by various artists.

🔲 D5 ✉ Shop 13, East Circular Quay, Opera Quays ☎ 9251 0511 🚇 Circular Quay

ARGYLE GALLERY

argylegallery.com.au

Fine Australian and Aboriginal arts and crafts sourced directly from the artists. Paintings, hand-blown glass, bronze animal sculptures, turned wood bowls and boxes, plus some unusual gift ideas, are displayed in a Victorian row house.

🔲 D5 ✉ 21 Playfair Street, The Rocks ☎ 9247 4427 🚇 Circular Quay

THE AUSTRALIAN WINE CENTRE

auswine.com.au

Choose from more than 1,000 Australian wines on sale here, including a good range of vintages. They will happily deliver to your hotel, or arrange overseas delivery.

🔲 D5 ✉ 42 Pitt Street ☎ 9247 2755 🚇 Circular Quay

CHOCOLARTS

chocolarts.com.au

Handcrafted chocolates and beautiful edible gifts are made on site using quality ingredients, including Belgian chocolate and natural Australian flavors.

🔲 D5 ✉ 75 George Street, The Rocks ☎ 9817 4222 🚇 Circular Quay

CRAFT NSW

artsandcraftsnsw.com.au

The Society of Arts and Crafts of NSW sells a range of work by its members at this gallery in the old Coroner's Court. You'll find contemporary Australian craft at its imaginative best.

🔲 D5 ✉ 12 Argyle Place, Millers Point ☎ 9241 5825 🚇 Circular Quay

KEN DUNCAN GALLERY

kenduncan.com

Ken Duncan, one of Australia's finest landscape photographers, captures Australia's natural scenery in stunning wide-format images. Framed original works are on display, as well as books of photographs.

🔲 D5 ✉ 73 George Street, The Rocks ☎ 9241 3460 🚇 Circular Quay

OPAL MINDED

opalminded.com

The family-owned Jundah mines in Queensland are the source of the black, boulder, light and crystal pipe opals sold here. You can buy individual stones or rings, pendants, earrings and cufflinks in distinctive gold or silver settings.

🔲 D5 ✉ 55 George Street, The Rocks ☎ 9247 9885 🚇 Circular Quay

THE ROCKS

therocks.com

In The Rocks Centre and on George Street you can buy original artwork, jewelry and other Australian crafts.

🔲 D5 ✉ The Rocks Heritage and Visitor Centre ☎ 9255 1788 🚇 Circular Quay

THE SHOPPER HOPPER

Combine the best of scenic Sydney with the best of outlet shopping and dining by booking a ticket on the Shopper Hopper (tel 1800 326 822, shopperhopper.com.au), an exclusive direct shopping ferry. Board at Darling Harbour or Circular Quay for a scenic 20-minute cruise past iconic Sydney landmarks on your way to two major shopping destinations, with top international and Australian brands.

THE ROCKS CENTRE

A well-designed complex specializing in Australiana, Aboriginal items, arts and crafts and souvenirs.

D5 ⊠ Argyle Street ☎ 9240 8500
🚋 Circular Quay

THE ROCKS MARKET

More than 150 stalls sell gifts, home-ware, antiques and jewelry, with plenty of cafés and free entertainment.

D5 ⊠ George Street ☎ 9240 8717
🕐 Fri 10–4, Sat–Sun 10–5 🚋 Circular Quay

SQUIDINKI

squidinkicom

Silk scarves, mugs, plates and bags with drawings of Sydney icons are for sale.

D5 ⊠ Shop 1, 21 Nurses Walk, The Rocks
☎ 9241 6112 🕐 Daily 10–6 🚌 339

AUSTRALIANA

If you are looking for souvenirs to take home, go for high-quality Australiana. You will find books on Australia, Aboriginal crafts and superb gemstones and jewelry.

Entertainment and Nightlife

THE ARGYLE

theargylerocks.com

Featuring six bars over two levels, and a cobblestoned courtyard, the historic Argyle continues to draw crowds with its DJs, open mike comedy nights, happy hours and contemporary pub menu.

C5 ⊠ 18 Argyle Street, The Rocks
☎ 9247 5500 🕐 Daily 11am–late 🚌 311

BLU BAR ON 36

This pricey 36th-floor cocktail bar in one of the city's top hotels provides elegance with astounding views.

D5 ⊠ Shangri-la Hotel, 176 Cumberland Street, The Rocks ☎ 9250 6000 🕐 Daily
🚌 311

LORD NELSON BREWERY HOTEL

lordnelsonbrewery.com

A visit to one of Sydney's oldest pub is a must—drinks have been served in this sandstone building since 1841.

C5 ⊠ 19 Kent Street, The Rocks ☎ 9251 4044 🕐 Daily 🚌 431, 432, 433

MERCANTILE HOTEL

themercantilehotel.com.au

This high-spirited Irish pub is in the Rocks Hotel, famous for its art deco wall tiles, Irish music and Guinness.

D4 ⊠ 25 George Street, The Rocks
☎ 9247 3570 🕐 Daily 🚋 Circular Quay

TANK STREAM BAR

This hidden bar is the perfect getaway for good wine and well-crafted cocktails.

D5 ⊠ 1 Tank Stream Way ☎ 9240 3100
🕐 Mon–Thu 4–late, Fri noon–late, Sat 5–late
🚋 Circular Quay

MODERN AUSTRALIAN

Australian cuisine is influenced by the eating habits of migrant Italians, Thais, Chinese and other nationalities. The cooking style might blend French and Thai, or local fish with Lebanese ingredients, to create a great dining experience. Bush tucker—such as kangaroo, crocodile and native plants—is another interesting option.

Where to Eat

PRICES	
Prices are approximate, based on a 3-course meal for one person.	
$$$	over A$60
$$	A$40–A$60
$	under A$40

ARIA ($$$)

For top-quality dining in a spectacular setting on the Harbour edge, try Aria. Chef owner Matt Moran's award-winning menus, exquisitely presented food and extensive wine list combine to create an occasion to savor.

🚇 D5 ✉ 1 Macquarie Street, East Circular Quay ☎ 9240 2255 🕐 Mon–Fri lunch, dinner daily, also pre-theater and supper menus 🚉 Circular Quay

CAFE SYDNEY ($$$)

cafesydney.com

Overlooking Circular Quay, this lively cocktail bar serves innovative Australian food and great desserts.

🚇 D5 ✉ Level 5, Customs House, Alfred Street ☎ 9251 8683 🕐 Mon–Fri and Sun lunch, Mon–Sat dinner 🚉 Circular Quay

CRUISE BAR ($$)

cruisebar.com.au

Sgnature cocktails, alfresco setting, tasty Modern Australian food and live entertainment in a classy yet casual setting.

🚇 D5 ✉ Level 1, Overseas Passenger Terminal, West Circular Quay ☎ 9251 1188 🕐 Daily 11am–late 🚉 Circular Quay

EST ($$$)

merivale.com.au/est

The grand dining room, immaculate service and innovative Australian cuisine highlighting Asian tastes make this the perfect place to celebrate that special occasion.

🚇 D5 ✉ Level 1, 252 George Street, The Rocks ☎ 9240 3010 🕐 Mon–Sat dinner 🚉 Town Hall

THE FINE FOOD STORE ($)

finefoodstore.com

If you want to try classic, modern Australian brunch fare, try it here. There's carefully made coffee and colorful meals like avocado bagels and eggs with spanner crab and bottarga.

🚇 C5 ✉ Corner of Kendall and Mill Lane, The Rocks ☎ 9252 1196 🕐 Mon–Sat 7am–4pm, Sun 7.30am–4pm 🚌 311

MCA CAFÉ ($$)

mca.com.au

Modern Australian menu with delicious seafood dishes, soups, salads, sandwiches and a kids' menu, plus there's a comprehensive wine list and great views of the Harbour. The best tables are on the Sculpture terrace.

🚇 D5 ✉ MCA, 140 George Street, The Rocks ☎ 9250 8443 🕐 Daily 10–4 (Thu to 9pm) 🚉 Circular Quay

MR WONG ($$)

merivale.com.au/mrwong

You can be sure to get authentic Cantonese dishes and the best dim sum in town in this big and popular restaurant with colonial-style decor.

🚇 D5 ✉ 3 Bridge Lane ☎ 9240 3000 🕐 Daily lunch and dinner 🚉 Wynyard

NEPTUNE PALACE ($$–$$$)

neptunepalace.com

Come here for good Chinese/Malaysian cuisine with dishes such as *lakas*, Malay curries, Penang-style chicken and tasty seafood dishes.

🚇 D5 ✉ Level 1, Gateway Building, corner Pitt and Alfred streets, Circular Quay ☎ 9241 3338 🕐 Daily lunch, dinner 🚉 Circular Quay

PONY DINING ($$$)

ponydiningtherocks.com
Situated in Sydney's oldest laneway, this handsome space, with an open kitchen, serves finessed dishes based on Australian produce and a wood-fired grill.
🚇 C5 ✉ Corner of Argyle Street and Kendall Lane, The Rocks ☎ 9252 7797 🕐 Daily lunch, dinner 🚌 311

Q DINING ($$$)

pullmanquaygrand
sydneyharbour.com
Enjoy great Circular Quay views while dining in this light and airy contemporary restaurant. Indigenous spices enhance local cuisine.
🚇 E5 ✉ Pullman Quay Grand Sydney Harbour ☎ 9256 1010 🕐 Daily breakfast, Mon–Fri lunch, Sat dinner, Sat–Sun high tea 🚢 Circular Quay

QUAY ($$$)

quay.com.au
On the S. Pellegrino World's 50 Best Restaurants list, award-winning Quay specializes in seafood. Fantastic Harbour views.
🚇 D5 ✉ Upper level, Overseas Passenger Terminal, Circular Quay West ☎ 9251 5600 🕐 Mon–Fri lunch, daily dinner 🚢 Circular Quay

QUAY BAR ($)

quaybar.com.au
Quay Bar has excellent food, boutique tap beers, imaginative cocktails, friendly staff and an international range of wines to go with the house salads, burgers, pies and bistro fare.
🚇 D5 ✉ Ground floor, Customs House, Alfred Street, Circular Quay ☎ 9247 4898 🕐 Mon–Fri 7.30am–late, Sat 9am–1am 🚢 Circular Quay

ROCKPOOL BAR & GRILL ($$–$$$)

rockpool.com
Rockpool continues its reign as Sydney's best seafood restaurant, with chef Neil Perry presenting his signature dishes with flair. Oysters are served in the bar.
🚇 D6 ✉ 66 Hunter Street ☎ 9252 1888 🕐 Mon–Fri lunch, Mon–Sat dinner 🚉 Wynyard

SAKÉ ($$)

sakerestaurant.com.au
Atmospheric and understated, this award-winning restaurant is popular for its traditional yet innovative Japanese cuisine. Dine light at the sushi bar or let the chefs curate your meal.
🚇 C5 ✉ 12 Argyle Street, The Rocks ☎ 9259 5656 🕐 Daily lunch, dinner 🚌 311

SIR STAMFORD AT CIRCULAR QUAY ($$)

stamford.com.au
The fabulously indulgent Sydney High Tea is served among the antiques of this elegant boutique hotel. The tea is a delicious mix of savory and sweet offerings, with a menu to dream about and ponder over. Reservations for High Tea are essential.
🚇 D5 ✉ 93 Macquarie Street ☎ 9252 4600 🕐 High tea served daily from 11am, last booking 4pm 🚢 Circular Quay

WILD GINGER DINING + BAR ($$)

wildgingerdiningbar.com.au
Set in a beautiful sandstone building, Wild Ginger fuses classic Thai flavors with Australian native ingredients in flavor-packed dishes, including vegan and vegetarian versions.
🚇 D5 ✉ 106 George Street, The Rocks ☎ 8283 8275 🕐 Mon–Fri lunch, daily dinner 🚌 399

Darling Harbour and Pyrmont

As the recreational hub of the city, Darling Harbour and Pyrmont are very busy on the weekends, when families come to enjoy the exhibitions, attractions and entertainment on offer.

Top 25

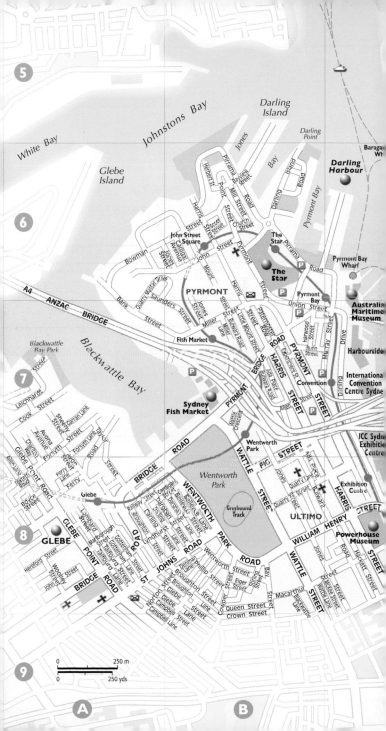

Barangaroo

P

Shelly Avenue

Lime St

A4 WESTERN DISTRIBUTOR

P

Erskine Street

Kent Street

Sussex Street

Wild Life Sydney Zoo

KING STREET

Sussex Street

P

Sea Life Sydney Aquarium

P

rmont ridge

P

Darling Park

DRUITT STREET

Kent Street

BATHURST STREET

Sussex Street

Kent Street

P

Darling Quarter

STREET

Tumbalong Park

Chinese Garden of Friendship and Chinatown

heatre

HARBOUR

Dixon Street

Sussex Street

P

GOULBURN

STREET

GEORGE STREET

ER STREET

Harbour Street

P

Little Hay Street

Sussex Street

Cunningham Street

Paddy's Markets

Darling Drive

Quay Street

Thomas Street

Hay Street

Campbell Street

Capitol Square

Ultimo

mbus Lane

C

D

E

Australian Maritime Museum

HIGHLIGHTS

- HMAS *Vampire*
- Hands-on exhibits
- Vietnamese refugee boat
- HMB *Endeavour*
- US Gallery
- Navy submarine
- *Spirit of Australia*

This comprehensive display of Australia's maritime heritage, from the arrival of the First Fleet to the modern voyages of Vietnamese boat people, documents Australia's links with the ocean.

Indoor displays The museum features eight themed sections—Eora: First People, Navigators, On the Waterfront, Commerce, Passengers, Sport and Play, Navy and Linked by the Sea—that contain thousands of items in displays as diverse as early beach fashions, the globe-circling yacht *Blackmore's First Lady* and migrant voyages. Other highlights include a section on Aboriginal and Torres Strait Islander people and the sea, the maritime links between Australia and the US and an intriguing display on how a Sydney man, Ken Warby, built the

Clockwise from left: entrance to the museum; interior exhibition space; the museum's waterside location

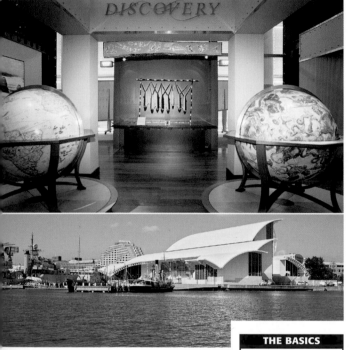

world's fastest boat, the *Spirit of Australia,* in his back garden. Temporary exhibitions are also presented regularly.

Outdoor displays Once you've seen what's on offer inside, go to the outdoor displays, moored at the museum's wharves. The historic vessels include HMAS *Vampire,* the last of the Royal Australian Navy's big gunships, and HMAS *Onslow,* one of the navy's submarines, both of which you can tour. Among other interesting craft are the *Akarana,* an 1888 racing cutter, a Vietnamese refugee boat that reached northern Australia, a lugger from the pearling port of Broome in Western Australia and *Krait,* used in a commando operation in World War II. A replica of HMB *Endeavour,* Captain Cook's famous vessel, is often moored for visitors to explore.

THE BASICS

anmm.gov.au

➕ C6

✉ 2 Murray Street, Darling Harbour

☎ 9298 3777

🕐 Daily 9.30–5 (to 6pm in Jan)

🍴 Good café, picnic tables

🚆 Town Hall; tram Light Rail to Pyrmont Bay

🚌 443

⛴ Pyrmont Bay Wharf

♿ Excellent

✋ Galleries: expensive; Big Ticket: expensive

❓ The Store book and gift shop

Chinese Garden of Friendship and Chinatown

Cantonese-style pavilions in the Chinese Garden of Friendship; celebrating Chinese New Year

THE BASICS

darlingharbour.com/things-to-do/chinese-garden-of-friendship

➕ C8

✉ Chinese Garden, Pier Street, Darling Harbour

☎ Chinese Garden 9240 8888

🕐 Daily Apr–Sep 9.30–5; Oct–Mar 9.30–5.30

🍴 Cafés and restaurants nearby

🚇 Town Hall

🚌 333, 433

🚊 Light rail to Paddy's Market Station

🚢 King's Wharf, Darling Harbour

♿ Good

💵 Inexpensive

HIGHLIGHTS

● Garden's pavilions, lakes and waterfalls
● Paddy's Markets (▷ 63)
● Dixon Street
● Capitol Theatre (▷ 64)

TIP

● Check out the many specialty shops for Asian cooking ingredients and herbal remedies.

The vibrant Chinese quarter, part of the city since the 1860s, is a great place for Asian cuisines and specialty shopping. The Chinese Garden, just a few steps from Chinatown, offers a calm retreat in the middle of busy downtown Sydney.

The Chinese Garden The largest of its kind outside mainland China, this tranquil garden was designed by Chinese landscape architects from Guangdong Province, a New South Wales sister state, and features Cantonese-style pavilions, lakes, waterfalls and bridges. With its shrubs, flowers and trees, including maples, this is a delightful spot in which to relax after seeing Darling Harbour's myriad attractions. Its other name is the Garden of Friendship, symbolizing the enduring links between China and Australia. The garden offers a calm retreat from the hustle and bustle of the city. A teahouse serves traditional Chinese tea, dim sum and other refreshments.

Chinatown On Dixon, Hay and Sussex streets, Sydney's Chinatown is a bustling area of Asian food and clothing shops and restaurants. Paddy's Markets are held here from Thursday to Sunday. The 1928 Capitol Theatre, home of major musical and theatrical events, is nearby on Campbell Street; it's worth seeing a show to appreciate its ornate interior. Chinese New Year (January or February) is an exciting time to be in the area, when you'll see fireworks, dragon dances and street processions.

DARLING HARBOUR AND PYRMONT TOP 25

Sydney's most innovative museum is housed in a cavernous old power station with modern extensions. Interactive audiovisual displays are combined with fascinating historical exhibits.

The building During the 1980s the 1899 Ultimo Power Station was transformed into Sydney's largest museum. Displays are housed in the vast boiler, turbine and engine houses, as well as the Neville Wran Building, inspired by grand 19th-century halls and rail stations.

The collection The award-winning museum contains much of the Museum of Applied Arts and Sciences' extensive collection. The contents range from the enormous 18th-century Boulton and Watt steam engine to historic gowns, from transport to ecology for a sustainable future, nuclear matters, cyberworlds, shopping in Australia 1880–1930, experiments in scientific principles and computers. There are also audio-visual presentations, sound effects, holograms and dozens of hands-on scientific displays. You can even sit in King's Cinema, a re-creation of a 1930s art deco cinema and watch a silent movie, accompanied by the bells, whistles and gadgetry of an electrically and air-activated Foto-player. Visit the shop for its range of books, gifts and interesting souvenirs.

Children welcome The museum is a wonder-land for youngsters, with many activities and hands-on explorations.

THE BASICS

powerhouse
museum.com

🚩 C8

✉ 500 Harris Street, Ultimo

☎ 9217 0111

🕐 Daily 10–5

🍴 Two cafés

🚆 Central; tram Light Rail to Paddy's Markets

🚌 501, M30

⛴ Aquarium Wharf, Darling Harbour

♿ Excellent

✋ Moderate

HIGHLIGHTS

● Decorative Arts section
● Boulton and Watt engine
● King's Cinema
● "Space: Beyond this World"
● Transportation section
● Cyberworlds
● Free WiFi

Sea Life Sydney Aquarium and Darling Harbour

HIGHLIGHTS

- Sharks in "The Open Ocean"
- Great Barrier Reef display
- Saltwater crocodiles
- Touch pool
- Marine Mammal Sanctuary
- Pyrmont Bridge

TIP

- The Aquarium can be crowded on weekends and during school holidays.

Encounter sharks and crocodiles at close quarters, marvel at the species diversity of the Great Barrier Reef and explore Australia's marine environments at this world-class aquarium.

Aquatic fun The real thrill here is walking through transparent plastic tunnels beneath the two vast floating oceanariums, watching schools of magnificent tropical fish, rays, eels and sharks glide above you. Look out for the Great Barrier Reef display, with its fish and vivid-colored coral. You can get up close with King and Gentoo penguins, marvel at the dugongs and meet the fish of Sydney Harbour.

Darling Harbour The eastern part of Darling Harbour offers several attractions, including the

Children watching sharks in Sea Life Sydney Aquarium (left); the twinkling lights of Darling Harbour at dusk (below)

IMAX Theatre, with the world's biggest screen, reopening after refurbishment in 2019.

Cockle Bay Wharf On the city side of Darling Harbour is a food and entertainment precinct, open daily until late. To the north of Cockle Bay there's Wild Life Sydney Zoo (▷ 62), next to the Aquarium. Here you'll see more than 6,000 Australian animals living in their natural habitats and some of Australia's deadliest snakes. Have lunch at King Street Wharf, a few minutes' walk farther north. Nearby Pyrmont Bridge (1902), which links the two sides of Darling Harbour, is the world's oldest electrically operated swing-span bridge and is still in use. Across the bridge is the Australian Maritime Museum (▷ 56–57) on your right, and Harbourside (▷ 63), a huge dining and shopping complex, on your left.

THE BASICS

sydneyaquarium.com.au

✚ C6, C7

✉ Sydney Aquarium and Wild Life Sydney Zoo, Aquarium Pier. IMAX Theatre, Aquarium Wharf, Darling Harbour

☎ Aquarium: 1 800 199657 (daily 9–5); Wild Life Sydney Zoo: 9333 9288; IMAX Theatre: 9281 3300

🕐 Aquarium daily 9.30–7; IMAX Theatre daily 10–10

🍴 Aquarium cafés

🚆 Town Hall; tram Light Rail to Convention Centre

🚌 Any bus to Market or King Street

⛴ Aquarium Wharf

♿ Very good

💰 Expensive

More to See

GLEBE

Glebe offers offbeat shopping, a Saturday market and the superb Nicholson Museum with its famous archaeological collection at the University of Sydney.

➕ A8 ☎ Museum 9351 2812 🕐 Museum Mon–Fri 10–4.30; closed public holidays 🍴 Cafés and restaurants 🚌 413 💲 Free

THE STAR

star.com.au

A vast and glittering entertainment venue with views of the Harbour and city, The Star boasts a huge range of restaurants, bars and cafés, nightclubs, upscale shops and a luxuriously appointed casino floor. Here, gamblers can try their luck at blackjack, roulette, poker, *pai gow*, *mah jong*, baccarat and 1,500 slot machines. The 2,000-seat Lyric Theatre (▷ 64) is also here, plus a sparkling rooftop Event Centre that hosts international stars and A-list acts in concert settings.

➕ B6 ✉ 80 Pyrmont Street, Pyrmont ☎ 9777 9000 🕐 Daily 24 hours

🍴 Numerous restaurants and cafés 🚆 Town Hall; tram Light Rail to The Star 🚌 43 🚢 Pyrmont Bay Wharf 💲 Free entry

SYDNEY FISH MARKET

Come to admire (and buy if you are going to a barbecue!) the vast range of fresh seafood and to sample the great fish and French fries. Also fruit, vegetables and deli items.

➕ B7 🚇 Corner of Pyrmont Bridge Road and Bank Street, Pyrmont ☎ 9660 1611 🕐 Daily 7–4 🚆 Tram Light Rail to Fish Market 🚌 443, 501

WILD LIFE SYDNEY ZOO

wildlifesydney.com.au

Some 6,000 Australian animals, including wallabies, possums, quolls, koalas and many deadly snakes, are housed in 10 replicated habitats. Check the website for daily feeding times and informative talks.

➕ C6 ✉ 1–5 Wheat Road, Sydney ☎ 1800 206 158 🕐 Daily 10–5 🚌 All buses to King Street 🚆 Tram Light Rail to Convention or Pyrmont Bay 🚢 Aquarium Pier 💲 Expensive

Browsing round Glebe Market

Catch of the day at the Sydney Fish Market

Shopping

BALMAIN MARKET

balmainmarket.com.au

With shoppers ranging from punks to aging hippies, this market (held on the grounds of an old church) has a pleasant community feel. Browse for arts and crafts and try the vegetarian food in the church hall.

B4 ⊠ Corner of Darling Street and Curtis Road, Balmain ☎ 9818 1791 ⏰ Sat 8.30–4 🚌 442, 445 🚢 Darling Street

CHINATOWN AND HAYMARKET

This area is home to many Asian food shops, dozens of cafés and restaurants and inexpensive clothes stores. Lively and cosmopolitan.

C8 ⊠ South of Goulburn Street 🚆 Central

CROCODILE SHOP

darlingharbour.com/shop/crocodile-shop.aspx

Possum, alpaca and merino wool feature with sheepskin, crocodile and kangaroo skin products that range from bags to belts, hats and wraps.

C7 ⊠ Level 1, shop 113, Harbourside, Darling Harbour ☎ 9211 7920 🚊 Tram Light Rail to Pyrmont Bay 🚆 Central

GLEBE MARKETS

glebemarkets.com.au

Around 200 outdoor stalls with clothing and fashion items, crafts and collectibles. Many interesting shops and some great cafés are nearby.

B9 ⊠ Glebe Public School, Glebe Point Road, Glebe ☎ 0419 291 449 ⏰ Sat 10–4 🚌 431, 433

GLEEBOOKS

gleebooks.com.au

An excellent bookshop in the inner-west suburb of Glebe, close to the University of Sydney. Great for browsing.

Gleebooks (Kids), also in Glebe Road, specializes in children's books.

B9 ⊠ 49 Glebe Point Road, Glebe ☎ 9660 2333 🚌 431

HARBOURSIDE DARLING HARBOUR

harbourside.com.au

Darling Harbour's shopping complex is vast—more than 150 shops, selling fashion items, souvenirs, CDs and tapes, jewelry and many other goods.

C7 ⊠ Darling Harbour ☎ 8204 1888 🚊 Tram Light Rail to Pyrmont Bay

PADDY'S MARKETS

paddysmarkets.com.au

Sydney's biggest and oldest market, with more than 1,000 stalls under cover, sells everything from clothes and books to jewelry and vegetables. Great for bargain hunters.

C8 ⊠ Corner of Thomas and Hay streets, Haymarket ☎ 9325 6200 ⏰ Wed–Sun 9–5 🚊 Tram Light Rail to Paddy's Markets

SUSSEX CENTRE

Excellent food court for a wide range of inexpensive Asian meals, plus Chinese herbalists, reflexology areas, Asian antiques and crafts and shops with exotic cooking ingredients and homewares.

C8 ⊠ 401 Sussex Street, Haymarket ☎ 9281 6388 🚌 443 🚊 Tram Light Rail to Capitol Square

THAI-KEE SUPERMARKET

An Asian supermarket in Chinatown, featuring a butcher's section, exotic fruit and vegetables, and spices and ingredients for Chinese, Malaysian, Thai and Vietnamese cooking.

C8 ⊠ Market City, 9–13 Hay Street ☎ 9211 3150 🚆 Central

Entertainment and Nightlife

CAPITOL THEATRE

capitoltheatre.com.au

Refurbishment has made the 2,000-seat Capitol, dating from 1928, Sydney's most glorious performance space. It's the home of musicals and major theatrical events.

🔢 D8 ✉ 13 Campbell Street, Haymarket ☎ 1300 558 878 🚇 Central (Railway Square exit)

CARGO BAR AND LOUNGE

cargobar.com.au

thecargolounge.com.au

Enjoy a sunset beer or cocktail in the outdoor beer garden or the split-level, waterside bar. On Friday you can dance from dusk until dawn.

🔢 C7 ✉ 52–60 The Promenade, King Street Wharf ☎ 8070 2424 ⏰ Daily 11am–late 🚇 Town Hall 🚌 412, 413 ⛴ Aquarium Pier

CHERRY

star.com.au

A cocktail bar with sparkling city views, tasty bar snacks that range from charcuterie to fried chicken, and dance sounds that span house, disco, Balearic beat and lounge DJ mixes.

🔢 B6 ✉ Level 1, Casino, The Star, 80 Pyrmont Street ☎ 1800 700 700 ⏰ Wed–Thu 5pm–12, Fri 4pm–1am, Sat 4pm–2am 🚊 Tram Light Rail to The Star ⛴ Pyrmont Bay Wharf

HARBOUR JET

harbourjet.com

Extreme Harbour tours by jet boat. Choose from the 35-minute Jet Blast Adventure (includes spins and power brake stops) or the slightly more sedate 50-minute Sydney Harbour Adventure. Photo opportunities and music.

🔢 C7 ✉ 50B The Promenade, King Street Wharf ☎ 1300 887 373 ⏰ Daily 🚇 Convention

HOME

homesydney.com

Several bars, views of Darling Harbour and, best of all, dance floors on three levels, featuring funk, house, techno and garage.

🔢 C7 ✉ 101/1 Wheat Road, Cockle Bay Wharf, Darling Harbour ☎ 9266 0600 ⏰ Fri–Sun; see website for events 🚇 Town Hall

PONTOON

pontoonbar.com

This bar and nightclub overlooking Darling Harbour has futuristic decor and a waterside restaurant open for lunch and dinner. Pontoon Fridays sees DJs spinning house, hiphop and RnB from 6pm. Check website for drinks specials.

🔢 C7 ✉ The Promenade, Cockle Bay Wharf, Darling Harbour ☎ 9267 7099 ⏰ Daily 11.30am–late 🚇 Town Hall

SYDNEY LYRIC

sydneylyric.com.au

This modern theater presents big musicals and a variety of internationally acclaimed performances.

🔢 B6 ✉ Pirrama Road, Pyrmont ☎ 9509 3600; tickets 1300 795 267 🚌 443 🚊 Tram Light Rail to The Star

---

BEERS AND BARS

Australia's beer scene has come on leaps and bounds in recent years, with a large craft beer movement happening in most capital cities. Larger, more ubiquitous brands you're likely to see on tap include Coopers, Boags, James Squire and Mountain Goat. Beer is generally served in "middies" (284ml/10fl oz glasses) and larger "schooners." Bars and pubs are licensed to trade for varying hours each day but are generally open until at least 11pm, while nightclubs and discos stay open longer.

Where to Eat

PRICES
Prices are approximate, based on a 3-course meal for one person. $$$ over A$60 $$ A$40–A$60 $ under A$40

BBQ KING ($$)

This Sydney institution is a must. Despite its relocation from its original Chinatown spot to glossier surrounds, you still can't beat it for late-night duck pancakes.

D8 ⊠ 76 78 Liverpool Street, Sydney ☎ 9267 2433 ⏰ Daily 10am–midnight ⊕ Town Hall 🚍 333, 394

EATING WORLD ($)

fishermanswharf.com.au

For a fast, cheap eat that satisfies any craving you may have for Asian food, head to this aptly named food court for dumplings, ramen or nasi lemak.

C8 ⊠ 25 29 Dixon Street, Haymarket ⏰ Daily 10–10 🚍 301

FISHERMAN'S WHARF ($)

fishermanswharf.com.au

You can handpick your seafood from the tanks of this Chinese restaurant. It has plenty to please meat-eaters, too.

B7 ⊠ Level 1, Bank Street, Pyrmont ☎ 9660 9888 ⏰ Daily lunch, dinner 🚍 443, 501

THE MALAYA ($–$$)

themalaya.com.au

One of the longest-established and best Asian restaurants in town, serving a tempting array of Indonesian, Malaysian and Chinese.

C6 ⊠ 39 Lime Street (Kings Street Wharf) ☎ 9279 1170 ⏰ Daily dinner, Mon–Sat lunch ⊕ Sydney Aquarium

MEJICO ($)

mejico.com.au

This colorful cantina takes a traditional Mexican menu and twists it into things like mushroom ceviche, cauliflower adobo tacos and tequila cured trout. Their tequila list is almost as long as the Harbour Bridge.

D6 ⊠ 105 Pitt Street, Sydney ☎ 9230 0119 ⏰ Mon–Sat 12pm–late ⊕ Wynyard

MOMOFUKU SEIOBO ($$$)

seiobo.momofuku.com

The Australian outpost of chef David Chang's celebrated Momofuku chain is an award-winning restaurant with an open kitchen and a degustation menu showcasing a winning mix of Caribbean flavors and Australian produce. There is also a bar area.

B6 ⊠ The Star, Level G, 80 Pyrmont Street, Pyrmont ☎ 9657 9169 ⏰ Mon–Sat 6pm–10pm 🚍 389

QUARRYMAN'S HOTEL ($)

quarrymanshotel.com.au

Up to 30 craft beers on tap—which change regularly—with bar food. There's a proper dining space upstairs offering seafood, burgers, steak, pies, pasta and nachos.

B7 ⊠ 216 Harris Street, Pyrmont ☎ 8710 3551 ⏰ Daily lunch, dinner 🚍 501

AUSTRALIAN SEAFOOD
Local specialties include Sydney rock oysters, while kingfish, enormous shrimps, Tasmanian scallops and smoked salmon, South Australian tuna and northern fish such as the delicious barramundi feature on menus all over town. Appropriately, many seafood restaurants have waterfront locations and also offer excellent take-out food.

CBD and East Sydney

The Central Business District is home to many major companies and associated financial and legal services, as well as the city's top hotels. Its retail heart includes charming old arcades, the imposing Queen Victoria Building and the major department stores.

Top 25

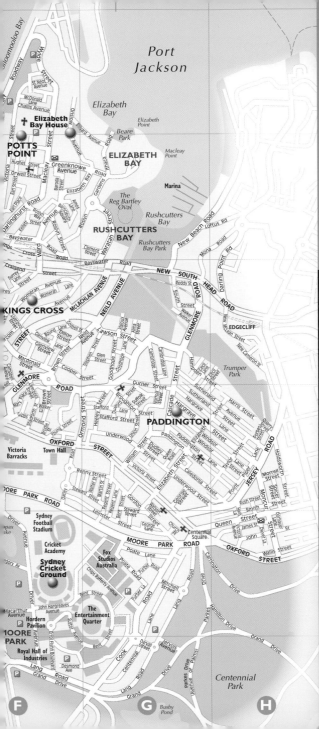

Art Gallery of New South Wales

HIGHLIGHTS

- Yiribana Gallery
- Thai bronze Buddhas (Asian Art room)
- Works by Margaret Preston
- Lloyd Rees's paintings
- Photography gallery
- Tom Roberts's paintings

The Aboriginal art is a particularly exciting part of the wonderful collection of Australian, Asian and European art exhibited here. The local works offer a wide-ranging view of Australian society and culture.

The collection The original Victorian building, located in The Domain, has been greatly extended to showcase the gallery's diverse permanent collection and regularly changing visiting international exhibitions. Besides work by European artists and notable Australian painters such as Frederick McCubbin, Arthur Streeton, Margaret Preston, Lloyd Rees, Tom Roberts and Sidney Nolan, the gallery has an excellent Asian art section, spread over two floors. European highlights include works by

Clockwise from left: impressive exhibition space; the colonnaded exterior of the museum; sculpture relaxing in the garden

Picasso, Van Gogh, Modigliani, Degas and Rodin. The prints and drawings room and the photography gallery are also well worth visiting. Watch out for the Sydney Modern Project—a spectacular expansion designed by the prize-winning architects SANAA and slated for completion in 2021 to coincide with the gallery's 150th anniversary.

The Yiribana Gallery The name means "this way" in the language of the Eora people. The gallery contains Australia's most comprehensive collection of Aboriginal and Torres Strait Islander art. More than 200 items, from contemporary paintings to sculptures and traditional works on bark, are housed here, representing artists from communities across Australia. The Yiribana Project Space hosts changing exhibitions.

THE BASICS

artgallery.nsw.gov.au

🔢 E6

✉ Art Gallery Road, The Domain

☎ 9225 1744; free infoline 1 800 679278

🕐 Daily 10–5 (Wed 10–10)

🍴 Excellent restaurant and café

🚉 St. James/Martin Place

🚌 441

♿ Excellent

💵 Free

❓ Free tours daily, lectures, performances and films; library and shop

Australian Museum

HIGHLIGHTS

- Aboriginal and Torres Strait collections
- Planet of Minerals room
- Eric
- Australian birds, especially the parrots
- Dinosaurs
- Skeleton Gallery
- Kidspace

TIP

- You can also spend a night in the museum. Take a flashlight and curl up with the dinosaurs!

Rated among the world's top natural history museums, the Australian Museum highlights the country's unique fauna and geology as well as the history of Australia's indigenous people.

The collection Housed in an 1849 building, with ever-evolving additions, the museum has an excellent Aboriginal area, a showcase of native birds, insects and mammals and an informative display on gems and minerals. One of the most interesting sections is the Skeleton Gallery, where the internal organs of various creatures, including a cycling human, can be examined. A must-see permanent exhibition, Dinosaurs brings the prehistoric world of predators and prey imaginatively to life with sounds and smells and even a projection of a dinosaur

Clockwise from top far left: the wonders of nature at the Australian Museum; getting down to the bare bones at the Skeleton Gallery; a lifelike model of ankylosaur Minmi *in the Dinosaurs exhibition; minerals on display in the Chapman Gallery; Search and Discover Gallery; facade of the museum; dinosaurs on display*

stampede. Don't miss Eric, a 110- to 120-million-year-old pliosaur; this opalized marine reptile was actually excavated far inland, at dusty Coober Pedy in South Australia.

Get involved The museum, of which Sir David Attenborough is a lifetime patron, offers tours and many options to get interactive. The Indigenous Tour includes a guided tour through the collection, bush tucker demonstrations and cultural performances.

Kidspace This area educates and intrigues under-5s. It features five "pods": bugs, marine life, volcanos, observation and imagination. Kids can feel animal skins, solve puzzles and listen to a story. Ask for a free ticket at the admissions desk when you buy your ticket.

THE BASICS

australianmuseum.net.au

➕ E7

✉ 1 William Street

☎ 9320 6000

🕐 Daily 9.30–5

🍴 Excellent café

Ⓜ Museum

🚌 311, 380, 382

♿ Very good

✋ Moderate

❓ Free tours daily; performances, special events and changing exhibitions; museum shop

City Centre

Archibald Fountain in Hyde Park (left); the fountain illuminated at night (below)

THE BASICS

cityofsydney.nsw.
gov.au

➕ D7

☎ Town Hall tours
9265 9333

🎫 Tours on demand

🚇 Town Hall, Museum

♿ Few

🎟 Free

HIGHLIGHTS

● Sydney Town Hall
● Harry Seidler buildings
● Hyde Park
● St. Andrews Cathedral
● Chifley Tower
● Archibald Fountain

TIP

● For quick luxury, pop into David Jones. Go past the pianist on the grand piano, and grab a seat at the iconic Oyster Bar in the Food Hall for oysters and champagne.

Many of Sydney's colonial-era and Victorian buildings have been lovingly restored and a walk around the city reveals some architectural gems. Don't forget the little backstreets.

Colonial and Victorian Sydney From its origins as a convict settlement, Sydney has always had fine public and commercial buildings. As the years went by and the population rapidly increased, many were progressively replaced with grander versions. Fortunately, a few colonial buildings, such as the Hyde Park Barracks (▷ 75) and St. James Church, remain, as do examples of 19th-century local sandstone architecture, such as the Town Hall in George Street, an elaborate 1869 building. You can look at the decorative vestibule and grand hall at any time, or join one of the tours that take place. Next door is St. Andrew's Cathedral (▷ 81), while St. Mary's Cathedral (▷ 81–82) is on the eastern side of Hyde Park.

Art deco Sydney A number of buildings survive, but the Anzac War Memorial (▷ 79), in the southern part of Hyde Park (▷ 80) and the Archibald Fountain, in the northern section, are the most accessible.

Modern Sydney Some of the city's modern buildings are worth finding: Chifley Tower (▷ 79) at Chifley Square and the Harry Seidler-designed buildings, the MLC Centre in Martin Place and Australia Square in George Street.

Hyde Park Barracks

This building, once home to convicts, was designed by the ex-forger turned architect Francis Greenway. Now a museum, it has remarkable displays covering convict life and Sydney's early years.

The barracks Located on historic Macquarie Street, Hyde Park Barracks (1819) is perhaps the city's most charming building. Standing in dignified seclusion behind its grand gates, this three-floor example of Georgian architecture originally accommodated convicts and later became a home for destitute women. The building is now a fascinating museum, focusing on the lives of these occupants and providing a glimpse into Sydney's early days. Changing exhibitions are mounted in the ground-floor Greenway Gallery. In 2019, to commemorate 200 years since the first convicts arrived at the Barracks, this UNESCO World Heritage-listed site launches a state-of-the-art transformation, with better accessibility and interactivity.

Queens Square and Macquarie Street
The city's most historically significant avenue, Macquarie Street, begins outside the barracks at Queens Square, which centers on an 1888 statue of Queen Victoria. This area contains the city's oldest church, the 1822 St. James (another Greenway building), and the 1816 Sydney Mint. To appreciate the street's charms, walk past Victorian Sydney Hospital, the Sydney Mint and State Parliament House (▷ 82), built in 1816, to the State Library (▷ 82).

THE BASICS

sydneylivingmuseums.com.au

🔒 E6

✉ Queens Square, Macquarie Street

☎ 8239 2311

🕐 Daily 10–5

🚇 Martin Place/St. James

🚌 200

⛴ Circular Quay

♿ Few

💲 Moderate

HIGHLIGHTS

● Elegant architecture
● Exhibitions in the Greenway Gallery
● Historic Macquarie Street
● St. James Church
● Statue of Queen Victoria

Paddington

HIGHLIGHTS

- Oxford Street
- Victoria Barracks
- Paddington Markets
- Terraced (row) houses
- Specialty shops
- Arthouse cinemas
- Art galleries

TIP

● Make the trip on a Saturday to coincide with the Paddington Markets.

Charismatic Paddington, a near city suburb of Victorian-era terraced (row) houses, straddles the eastern thoroughfare of Oxford Street, which is lined with an array of specialty shops.

Paddington's houses With their decorative wrought-iron balconies and fences, these are architectural gems. Built between the 1840s and the 1890s as middle-class housing, most have been restored to create a charming suburb, listed as a conservation area by the National Trust. Today, art galleries and antiques shops abound and walking is the perfect way to combine sightseeing, shopping and dining.

The suburb Paddington is divided by Oxford Street, which originates at Hyde Park in the

Clockwise from far left: the delightful terraced (row) houses of Paddington; Paddington Market is a great place to shop for a bargain; framed pictures on sale at the market; wrought-iron balconies are an attractive feature of many of Paddington's houses

CBD and runs through the gay district in Darlinghurst, through Paddington, to Bondi Junction. On Saturday, Paddington Markets (▷ 86) draws crowds to the specialty shops selling fashion, homewares, books and gifts. Cafés and restaurants cater for the hungry and thirsty, while two cinema complexes show art-house movies. Nearby is Centennial Park, an idyllic collection of open spaces.

Victoria Barracks This imposing National Trust listed sandstone-block building was constructed by soldiers and convicts in the 1840s as a bar-racks, and remains a military base today. The 226m (610ft) long facade sits imposingly in front of a large parade ground. Guided tours include the military museum and other sections of the base.

THE BASICS

sydney.com
✚ G9
✉ Victoria Barracks, Oxford Street
☎ 8335 5330
🕐 Thu 10–12.20. Tours by appointment first Sun of the month 10–3.30
🍽 Numerous cafés and restaurants
🚌 378, 380, 382
💶 Inexpensive; tours free

Sydney Tower and Skywalk

TOP 25

Sydney Tower and other skyscrapers (left); the tower seen from Hyde Park (below)

THE BASICS

sydneytowereye.com.au
🔲 D7
✉ Level 5, Westfield Sydney Shopping Centre, 100 Market Street
☎ 1 800 258693
🕐 Daily 9–9. Check website for scheduled variations
🍴 Revolving restaurants, coffee lounge
🚆 St. James/Town Hall
🚌 Any bus along George Street or Elizabeth Street
♿ Good
💷 Expensive

HIGHLIGHTS

● View of Sydney Harbour, the city buildings and south to Botany Bay
● Night views
● Revolving restaurants
● High-speed elevator
● Skywalk
● 4-D cinema

This 305m (1,000ft) high structure, soaring dizzyingly above the city, is the best place to view Sydney's layout. The incredible panorama from the tower's viewing levels extends to the Blue Mountains on a clear day.

The structure Completed in 1981, gold-topped Sydney Tower is anchored by 56 stabilizing cables. One of the tallest public buildings in the southern hemisphere, it contains two revolving restaurants, an observation level, a 4-D cinema and a coffee shop. A ride in one of the three high speed, double-deck elevators—a mere 40 seconds—is an experience in itself. High-powered binoculars on the enclosed Observation Deck bring the city's sights into close-up view. Zoom in on the Harbour's shoreline, check out some beachside playgrounds and focus in on aviation activity at Sydney's airport. Interactive touchscreens offer fast facts and useful information on famous landmarks. The 4-D Cinema Experience encapsulates many facets of the city through engaging film footage and special in-theater effects.

Skywalk Constructed at the top of Sydney Tower in 2005, the A$4million Skywalk is twice the height of the Sydney Harbour Bridge. The 45-minute guided tour around the outside of the Tower's golden turret offers an exciting, bird's-eye view of the city, especially when you look down through the Skywalk's glass-floor viewing platform. A visit after dark is magical.

More to See

ANZAC WAR MEMORIAL

anzacmemorial.nsw.gov.au

This huge 1934 art deco structure, decorated with poignant sculptures, is Sydney's tribute to all Australians who served their country in war. Inside, the domed ceiling is dotted with 120,000 stars representing each man and woman from New South Wales who served overseas in World War I.

➕ D7 ✉ Hyde Park South ☎ 8262 2900 ⏰ Daily 9–5 🍴 Nearby 🔲 Museum 🎟 Free

AUSTRALIAN CENTRE FOR PHOTOGRAPHY

acp.org.au

Australia's premier photography gallery, established in 1973, has two exhibition spaces, a project wall for emerging artists, a workshop with public access and a specialist bookshop. For interested practitioners there is a darkroom facility, a digital workstation and a research library. The excellent gallery is a nonprofit organization.

➕ E8 ✉ 72 Oxford Street, Darlinghurst ☎ 9332 0555 ⏰ Tue–Fri 10–5, Sat 11–4 🍴 Nearby 🚌 380 🎟 Free

BRETT WHITELEY STUDIO

artgallery.nsw.gov.au/brett-whiteley-studio

This museum and gallery, opened in 1995, is a tribute to Brett Whiteley, born in 1939, one of Australia's most important and controversial modern artists, who died of a drug overdose in 1993. His studio, now managed by the Art Gallery of NSW (▷ 70–71), is full of his sculptures, paintings, drawings and memorabilia.

➕ E10 ✉ 2 Raper Street, Surry Hills ☎ 9225 1881 ⏰ Fri–Sun 10–4 🍴 Nearby 🚌 302, 372 🎟 Free

CHIFLEY TOWER

chifley.com.au

With a recent refurbishment that echoes the art deco curves of the building, Chifley Tower is a gleaming structure of commerce, retail and dining. The shops are chic and the dining options are plentiful, with

The stunning staircase at Elizabeth Bay House (▷ 80)

The 1934 art deco Anzac War Memorial

the concept of a food court spruced up to a sophisticated level. There are stunning Harbour views to be had, too.

🚩 D6 ✉ Chifley Square ☎ 9221 4500 🕐 Daily 🍴 Cafés and restaurants 🚉 Martin Place 💷 Free

ELIZABETH BAY HOUSE

sydneylivingmuseums.com.au
Constructed from Sydney sandstone, the elegant Elizabeth Bay House was built between 1835 and 1839. The house's most important feature is its oval-shaped salon and winding staircase, regarded as Australia's finest. Rooms are open to the public and are furnished in Regency style.

🚩 F6 ✉ 7 Onslow Avenue, Elizabeth Bay ☎ 8239 2333 🕐 Fri–Sun 11–4 🍴 Nearby 🚉 Kings Cross 💷 Inexpensive

HYDE PARK

This CBD haven has been a park since 1810 and is a popular lunchtime spot for city workers. You can wander among formal gardens and tree-lined paths and visit the Anzac War Memorial (▷ 79).

🚩 D7 ✉ Off Elizabeth Street 🕐 Daily 🍴 Nearby 🚉 St. James 💷 Free

KINGS CROSS AND POTTS POINT

Once Sydney's most bohemian district, Kings Cross can be pretty sketchy at times, but gentrification is starting to creep in and there are some good cafés. Adjacent Potts Point (Macleay and Victoria streets in particular) has interesting old domestic architecture and cafés.

🚩 F8, F7 🍴 Many cafés and restaurants 🚉 Kings Cross 💷 Free

QUEEN VICTORIA BUILDING

qvb.com.au
The delightfully restored interior of Sydney's most imposing Victorian-era building prompted French fashion guru Pierre Cardin to describe the structure as "the most beautiful shopping center in the world." Constructed to commemorate Queen Victoria's Golden

Chill out at lunchtime in Hyde Park

The illuminated Archibald Fountain, Hyde Park

Jubilee, and completed in 1898, the domed Romanesque-style QVB was originally used to house markets downstairs and offices upstairs.

Capped by a central glass dome, the 200m (180ft) long building, occupying an entire city block and containing more than 180 shops, cafés and restaurants, features beautiful stained-glass windows, patterned floor tiles and period shades and appointments, while the four main floors are divided into elegant Victorian-fronted shops. The lower-level food court and ground-floor shops are more run-of-the-mill, but the upper floors contain outlets for international labels as well as excellent local designers and a wide range of quality souvenir shops. On Victoria Walk (second floor), there is an interesting collection of historical objects. Here you can admire a replica of the British Crown jewels, an incredibly ornate Chinese jade bridal carriage, the extraordinary "Royal Clock" and a jade tree.

🗺 D7 ✉ Corner of George, York, Market and Druitt streets ☎ 9264 9209 🕐 Mon–Sat shops generally 9–6 (Thu 9–9), Sun 11–5 🍴 Many food stalls, cafés and restaurants 🚉 Town Hall 🚌 Any Circular Quay-bound bus ♿ Very good 🎟 Free

ST. ANDREW'S CATHEDRAL
sydneycathedral.com
St. Andrew's, built in the Gothic Revival style and consecrated in 1868, is the mother church of the Anglican Diocese of Sydney. Visitors can look around inside and attend services (check website for times).
🗺 D7 ✉ Corner of George and Bathurst streets ☎ 9265 1661 🚉 Town Hall 🎟 Free

ST. MARY'S CATHEDRAL
stmaryscathedral.org.au
One of the finest 19th-century Gothic-Revival churches in the world, the church has impressive stained-glass windows and a stunning mosaic tile floor in the crypt. Free guided tours on Sunday at 12 follow the Solemn Choral Mass.

Exterior of the Queen Victoria Building

Stained-glass window in the State Library

🏛 E7 ✉ Corner of St. Mary's Road and College Street ☎ 9220 0400 🚇 St. James 🎟 Free

STATE LIBRARY OF NEW SOUTH WALES

sl.nsw.gov.au

More than just a library, this large complex has a good shop, talks, events, festivals, exhibitions (a small charge for some) and free tours.

🏛 E6 ✉ Macquarie Street ☎ 9273 1414 🕐 Mon–Thu 9–8, Fri 9–5, Sat–Sun 10–5 🍴 Licensed café 🚇 Martin Place 🎟 Free

STATE PARLIAMENT HOUSE

parliament.nsw.gov.au

Originally part of the Rum Hospital, Parliament House (built in 1816) is a fine example of early colonial architecture and features shady verandas. The building was extended during the 1970s and 1980s to meet the demands of a growing government administration. You can take a tour of the building, but it's best to make a reservation.

🏛 E6 ✉ Macquarie Street ☎ Tours 9230 2047 🕐 Tours: check website for dates 🍴 Nearby 🚇 Martin Place 🎟 Free

SYDNEY CRICKET GROUND

sydneycricketground.com.au

The famed SCG is the home of first-class cricket in New South Wales. Test and one-day matches are played in summer, or you can visit the stadium and its Cricket Museum on a tour—SGC Tour Experience (call 1300 724 737).

🏛 F10 ✉ Driver Avenue, Moore Park ☎ 9360 6601 🕐 See website for tour schedule 🚌 371–377, 392–399

WOOLLOOMOOLOO

This glitzy inner-city address has some quaint terraced (row) houses. On Cowper Wharf Road you will find the historic Finger Wharf that juts far out into the bay, ships of the Australian Navy's fleet and Artspace, a gallery of contemporary art.

🏛 F7 ✉ Artspace, 43–51 Cowper Wharf Road ☎ 9356 0555 🕐 Tue–Fri 11–5, Sat–Sun 11–6 🍴 Nearby 🚌 311 🎟 Free

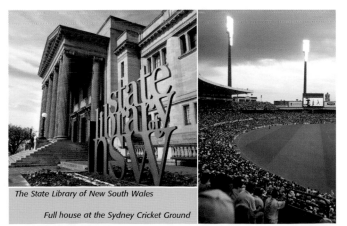

The State Library of New South Wales

Full house at the Sydney Cricket Ground

Paddington and Woollahra

Walk the backstreets of these two captivating inner-city suburbs to view the interesting architecture and check out the shops.

DISTANCE: 3km (2 miles) **ALLOW:** 45 minutes–2 hours

START

CNR OXFORD AND QUEEN STREETS
🔲 G10 🚌 378, 380

END

OXFORD STREET
🔲 G9 🚌 378, 380

① Paddington and Woollahra grew up around the 1841 Victoria Barracks (▷ 77) and by the 1880s was crammed with terraced (row) houses. With their iron lacework balconies, the brick-built terraces make Paddington unique and charming.

② From the intersection of Oxford Street turn left onto Queen Street, full of exclusive antiques shops. Take a left on to Moncur Street and walk down Hargrave Street.

③ You are now in the conservation area of Paddington listed by the National Trust. Turn left to Elizabeth Street, right to Paddington Street and right again on to Cascade Street.

⑦ This is home to Sydney's most interesting clothing shops as well as book, music and jewelry outlets. The Saturday Paddington Markets is held here (▷ 86).

⑥ Approximately 200m (180 yards) farther along Glenmore Road, turn left onto steep Ormond Street. Back on Oxford Street, turn left to reach the main Paddington shopping and café strip.

⑤ Continue along Glenmore Road to Five Ways.

④ Cascade Street has some particularly good examples of the local architecture, made in the local sandstone material. Walk down Cascade Street and head left on to Gurner Street.

CBD AND EAST SYDNEY WALK

83

Shopping

ADRIENNE & THE MISSES BONNEY

adrienne-bonney.com.au

This exclusive baby boutique sells the finest of the fine exquisite hand-made clothes, nursery gifts, an array of soft toys and bedtime garments.

🚹 J7 🖂 55 Bay Street, Double Bay ☎ 9363 1723 🚌 324, 325

AKIRA

akira.com.au

One of Australia's most celebrated designers, Akira Isogawa's soft, romantic, often richly embellished clothes take inspiration from the East.

🚹 D7 🖂 Level 2, Strand Arcade, 412 George Street ☎ 9232 1078 🚇 St James

BERKELOUW PADDINGTON

berkelouw.com.au

Selling new, used and rare books, this beloved bookstore also hosts book clubs and writers events, and has an excellent café and wine bar upstairs, where you can order coffee and crack open that new book.

🚹 D6 🖂 19 Oxford Street, Paddington ☎ 9360 3200 🕐 Sun–Thu 9.30am–10pm, Fri–Sat 9.30am–11pm 🚌 378, 380, 382

CASTLEREAGH STREET

This central street offers up-to-the-minute Louis Vuitton, Hermès, Chanel, Christian Lacroix and other major designer labels, as well as the chic MLC Centre opposite.

🚹 D6 🖂 Around where Castlereagh Street intersects with King Street 🚇 Martin Place

CHIFLEY PLAZA

chifley.com.au

This has a cluster of designer shops (along with a host of tempting dining options) in refurbished surrounds

inspired by the art deco style and sophistication of the building.

🚹 D6 🖂 Chifley Square ☎ 9229 0165 🚇 Martin Place

COUNTRY ROAD

countryroad.com.au

An Australian international success story, Country Road also has branches in the Queen Victoria Building, Bondi and Oxford Street, Paddington (as well as overseas). It sells countrified his and hers casual clothes as well as a range of home furnishings. Popular with bush and city dwellers alike.

🚹 D7 🖂 Corner of Pitt and King streets ☎ 9394 1818 🚇 Martin Place

DAVID JONES

davidjones.au

"DJs," Sydney's best department store, occupies two vast buildings. The Elizabeth Street branch is a breathtaking masterpiece of glass, marble and chrome. The Market Street branch has a wonderful food hall.

🚹 D7 🖂 Elizabeth Street and Market Street ☎ 9266 5544 🚇 St. James

DAVID JONES FOOD HALL

The lower level of this store is the city's most exclusive food store. You will find

---

AUSSIE DESIGN

Mambo (mambo-world.com) is famous for bright surf and streetwear carrying designs from the talented Reg Mombassa. Funky, translucent and cheerful best describes the jewelry and homewares at Dinosaur Designs (see opposite). The Strand Arcade (▷ 86) and major department stores David Jones (right) and Myer (🖂 436 George Street ☎ 9238 9111) stock Australia's top fashion designer labels.

the very finest produce here, including delicatessen lines, Australian wines, beers, cheeses, meats, seafood, fruit and vegetables.

⊞ D7 ✉ Market Street store, corner of Market and Castlereagh streets ☎ 9266 5544 🚇 St. James

DINOSAUR DESIGNS

dinosaurdesigns.com.au

Silver and semi-precious stones are used in offbeat and modern designs in this jewelry shop.

⊞ D7 ✉ Shop 77, Strand Arcade, Pitt Street Mall ☎ 9223 2953 🚇 St. James

DOUBLE BAY

This ritzy waterside suburb is a must for upscale Australian and overseas designer shopping—expensive clothes, shoes and leather goods—as well as antiques, books and jewelry. Don't miss Transvaal Avenue, with its interesting boutiques.

⊞ J7 🚌 324, 325

DYMOCKS

dymocks.com.au

Sydney's largest bookshop stocks books on every imaginable topic, as well as stationery. The Australian section near the entrance is very good and the best place to peruse titles on the country's bestseller list.

⊞ D6 ✉ 424–430 George Street ☎ 9235 0155 🚇 Town Hall

EQ VILLAGE MARKETS

Much of the fresh produce sold here is direct from the grower so it is well worth the 15-minute bus ride from the CBD.

⊞ F10 ✉ Entertainment Quarter, 122 Lang Road, Moore Park ☎ 9383 4163 🕐 Wed, Sat 8–2 🚌 371, 373, 376, 377

THE FAMILY JEWELS

thefamilyjewels.com.au

Beautifully designed contemporary gold, silver and other jewelry is set with semi-precious stones such as amethyst and turquoise. Its sister CBD store can be found in St. James Arcade, 80 Castlereagh Street.

⊞ F9 ✉ 48 Oxford Street, Paddington ☎ 9331 6647 🚌 378, 380, 382

HARDY BROTHERS

hardybrothers.com.au

An Australian gem specialist featuring exquisite Broome South Sea pearls, Argyle diamonds and fine opals. You will also find Swiss watches, silverware, china and a range of other high-quality items at this company that's been in business for more than 160 years.

⊞ D7 ✉ 60 Castlereagh Street ☎ 9232 2422 🚇 St. James

JUST WILLIAM CHOCOLATES

just william.com.au

This tiny shop, just off Paddington's Oxford Street, sells exquisite handmade chocolates. The chocolates and their customized designer packaging are legendary in Australia, where clients include A-list celebrities.

⊞ G9 ✉ 4 William Street, Paddington ☎ 9331 5468 🚌 378, 380, 382

MLC CENTRE

mlccentre.com.au

The MLC features everything from a food court to some of Sydney's most exclusive stores—international labels such as Gucci and Cartier are here, as are some of the top Australian designers. It also hosts Sydney's oldest theater, the Theatre Royal.

⊞ D6 ✉ 19 Martin Place ☎ 9224 8333 🚇 Martin Place

OBJECT SHOP

australiandesigncentre.com/object-shop
For something unique and a genuine souvenir of Australia, check out the Australian handmade craft and design pieces here at the Australian Design Centre's Object Shop, including jewelry, ceramics, artworks and glassware. You can often meet the makers in store on Saturdays.

🔛 E7 ✉ 113–115 William Street, Darlinghurst ☎ 9361 4555 🕐 Tue–Sat 11–4 🚌 301

PADDINGTON MARKETS

paddingtonmarkets.com.au
Held every Saturday come rain or shine, this is the trendiest market in town, featuring mostly clothing, accessories, arts, crafts and jewelry at good prices. The street performers are often very entertaining.

🔛 G9 ✉ Corner of Oxford and Newcombe streets, Paddington ☎ 9331 2923 🕐 Sat 10–4 (closes at 4pm in winter) 🚌 333, 378, 380

PASPALEY PEARLS

paspaley.com
Sydney's South Sea pearl specialist has outlets in Paris, Dubai and New York. Paspaley's northern Australian pearling company is regarded as the source of the finest pearls in the world.

🔛 D6 ✉ 2 Martin Place ☎ 9232 7633 🚇 Martin Place

QUEEN VICTORIA BUILDING

qvb.com.au
This imposing 1898 building with stained glass and tiled floors occupies an entire city block and is a delightful setting for beautifully appointed shops and cafés (▷ 80–81).

🔛 D7 ✉ Corner of George, York, Market and Druitt streets ☎ 9264 9209 🚇 Town Hall

RED EYE RECORDS

redeye.com.au
In business since 1981, this record store is Sydney's largest independent record store and an institution on the Sydney music scene. Head here for passionate service and an overwhelming range of Australian and international music, DVDs and ephemera.

🔛 D7 ✉ 143 York Street, Sydney ☎ 9267 7400 🕐 Mon–Sat 9–6, Sun 10–6 🚇 Central Station

R. M. WILLIAMS

rmwilliams.com.au
This legendary Bushman's Outfitters sells Australian country and Outback clothing, including moleskin pants, sturdy leather boots and Drizabone oilskin coats.

🔛 D7 ✉ 4 Westfield Sydney, 188 Pitt Street ☎ 9232 6904 🚇 St. James 🚇 Town Hall

THE STRAND ARCADE

strandarcade.com.au
This rebuilt historic arcade, originally dating from 1892, contains a number of shops across three levels, surrounded by decorative wrought ironwork and stained-glass windows. There are some good specialty shops, too.

🔛 D7 ✉ Pitt Street Mall and 412 George Street ☎ 9232 4199 🚇 St. James

ZOMP

zomp.com.au
Zomp started in Perth in the early 1970s and still brings edgy, designer shoes and a selection of stylish European footwear into their sleek, architectural stores. Stomp into Zomp for everything from black velvet pumps to blue glitter ankle boots.

🔛 F9 ✉ Shop 4, 255c Oxford Street, Paddington ☎ 9360 1546 🕐 Mon–Sat 9–6, Sun 10–6 🚌 333

Entertainment and Nightlife

ALLIANZ STADIUM

allianz.com.au/stadium

Rugby league, rugby union and soccer are played in this ultramodern stadium. Watch out for the new, futuristic version of the stadium, due to complete 2022.

🔲 F10 ✉ Driver Avenue, Moore Park
☎ 9360 6601 🚌 372, 373, 377, 393, 394, 396

ARQ

arqsydney.com.au

Dance music and drag shows are the name of the game at this premier LGBTQI nightspot on Flinders Street. Check the website for the schedule.

🔲 E8 ✉ 16 Flinders Street, Taylor Square
☎ 9380 8700 🕐 Thu–Sat 9pm–closure varies
🚌 378, 380

BELVOIR STREET THEATRE

belvoir.com.au

Company B, a long-running and critically acclaimed theater company, presents some of Australia's newest productions.

🔲 D9 ✉ 25 Belvoir Street, Surry Hills
☎ 9667 3444 🚉 Central

BURDEKIN HOTEL

burdekin.com.au

This popular hotel in Darlinghurst has a large bar on the Oxford Street side and the more intimate, expensive art deco Dug Out Bar on Liverpool Street.

🔲 E8 ✉ 2 Oxford Street, Darlinghurst
☎ 9331 3066 🕐 Wed–Fri 4pm–late, Sat 6pm–late 🚉 Museum

CENTENNIAL PARK

Perfect for cycling, horse riding, walking, and rollerblading. Horses and equipment can be rented. It's the summer home of the Moonlight Cinema (▷ 88).

🔲 H10 ✉ Off Oxford Street, Woollahra
☎ 9339 6699 🕐 Daily during daylight hours
🚌 378, 380, 382

COOPER PARK TENNIS COURTS

cptennis.com.au

Scenically, there is no better place for tennis than this bushland spot between Bondi Junction and Double Bay.

🔲 J9 ✉ 1 Bunna Place, off Suttie Road, Woollahra ☎ 9389 3100 🕐 Daily 🚉 Bondi Junction, then bus 330

DOWNTOWN

thecommons.com.au

The downstairs bar at The Commons pub/restaurant is in a great old sandstone building. The bar menu and music are inspired by the golden age of cocktails, jazz and blues.

🔲 E8 ✉ 32 Burton Street, Darlinghurst
☎ 9358 1487 🕐 Thu 6pm–midnight, Fri–Sat 6pm–1am 🚌 380, 382

ENTERTAINMENT QUARTER

eqmoorepark.com.au

This complex of cinemas, restaurants, shops and markets is Sydney's latest entertainment and dining hotspot. There are numerous activities to keep children occupied.

🔲 F10 ✉ Lang Road, Moore Park ☎ 8117 6700 🕐 Daily 10am–late. 🚌 372, 377, 390, 399

LGBTQI

Sydney is the home of the world's largest gay and lesbian parade—the Mardi Gras—which takes place in February or March. The area around lower Oxford Street (sometimes referred to as the Great Gay Way) is the heart of this alternative scene. Many hotels, bars and clubs here cater to the LGBTQI community; popular venues include Universal in Oxford Street (▷ 88), the Colombian Hotel (✉ 117–125 Oxford Street) and the Newtown Hotel (✉ 174 King Street, Newtown).

LORD DUDLEY

lorddudley.com.au

A very popular English-style pub, the Lord Dudley serves beer in pint as well as half-pint tankards. It has 18 local and imported beers on tap, shows sporting events on large screens and boasts open fires in the lounge in winter. The downstairs eating area serves Modern Australian food with a British twist.

🔢 H9 ✉ 236 Jersey Road, Woollahra ☎ 9327 5399 🕐 Daily 🚌 389

THE METRO

metrotheatre.com.au

This is Sydney's leading independent rock venue and a great place to catch a live band. Dance, comedy, fringe and other performances also feature from time to time. Check out The Lair downstairs, which hosts music, comedy nights and other live performances.

🔢 D8 ✉ 624 George Street ☎ 9389 3100 for performance information 🚇 Town Hall

MOONLIGHT CINEMA

moonlight.com.au

In summer, this open-air cinema screens previews, contemporary cult and classic movies on Centennial Park's Belvedere Amphitheatre lawns. Screenings start at sundown (around 8.30pm). Arrive early to grab one of the bean beds available for hire.

🔢 H10 ✉ Nearest gates, Woollahra Gates on Oxford Street, Paddington ☎ See website for ticket and performance information 🕐 Tue–Sun 7–11pm 🚌 378, 380, 382

MOORE PARK GOLF CLUB

mooreparkgolf.com.au

Easily accessible from the city, this club offers an 18-hole course, a 60-bay, all-weather day and night driving range, and all facilities at very reasonable rates.

🔢 F11 ✉ Corner of Anzac Parade and Cleveland Street, Moore Park ☎ 9663 1064 🕐 Golf course 8pm (summer), 6–5 (winter), driving range Mon 10am–11pm, Tue–Sun 6am–11pm 🚌 373, 374, 377, 394

ROYAL HOTEL

royalhotel.com.au

This charming hotel is known for its upstairs Elephant Bar, which has a great cocktail menu, and its Rooftop Bar, which is perfect for sunset drinks. The restaurant serves bistro meals.

🔢 G9 ✉ 257 Glenmore Road, Five Ways, Paddington ☎ 9331 2604 🕐 Mon–Sat 12–12, Sun 12–10 🚌 389

STATE THEATRE

statetheatre.com.au

This ornate 2,000-seat arena is the venue for musicals, ballet, the Sydney Film Festival and performances of live music. There are two-hour tours on Mon, Tue and Wed at 10am and 1pm.

🔢 D6 ✉ 49 Market Street ☎ 136 100 to book tours and for performance information 🚇 Town Hall

UNIVERSAL

universal.sydney

Picking up where the Midnight Shift left off, Universal is one of Sydney's most popular gay clubs, with drag, DJs and house music parties into the wee hours.

🔢 G9 ✉ 85–91 Oxford Street, Darlinghurst ☎ 8080 7065 🕐 Downstairs Fri–Sat 4pm–4am, upstairs Fri–Sun 9pm–4am 🚌 373, 301

ABORIGINAL DANCE

Bangarra Dance Company, which fuses contemporary and traditional dance routines into dramatic and exciting performances, can be seen at the Opera House and other venues.

Where to Eat

PRICES	
Prices are approximate, based on a 3-course meal for one person.	
$$$	over A$60
$$	A$40–A$60
$	under A$40

360 BAR AND DINING ($$$)

360dining.com.au

Enjoy fine dining in an elegant setting in the heart of the CBD, with ever-changing views of the city. The revolving 360 Bar & Dining at the top of the Sydney Tower offers dramatic decor and the skills of an award-winning head chef. There's a less expensive, family-friendly buffet restaurant atop the Tower, too.

⊞ D7 ⊠ Gallery Level 4, 4 Sydney Westfield Centre, Cnr Market Street and Pitt Street Mall ☎ 8223 3800 ⏲ Daily lunch, dinner 🚇 Town Hall

BALKAN SEAFOOD ($$)

balkanseafood.com.au

Order chargrilled octopus and fish at this old-school Croatian restaurant, which has been run by the same family since the early 1960s. Although famed for its seafood, meat-lovers have a good choice, including pasta dishes. BYO.

⊞ G9 ⊠ 249 Crown Street, Darlinghurst ☎ 9331 7670 ⏲ Daily 11.30am–late 🚌 380

BILLS ($)

bills.com.au

This is a popular breakfast and lunch spot for those on the run, long famous for the best scrambled eggs and ricotta hotcakes in town. Visitors and locals gather around a communal table, contributing to the buzzy atmosphere.

⊞ E8 ⊠ 433 Liverpool Street, Darlinghurst (also in Surry Hills) ☎ 9360 9631 ⏲ Daily breakfast, lunch 🚇 Museum

BISTRO MONCUR ($$–$$$)

woollahrahotel.com.au

Light, bright and luxurious, Bistro Moncur has stayed true to its French bistro roots, consistently serving up lush French classics like confit duck leg or chicken liver pâté with pickled cherries. There are two- and three-course set menus and a lunchtime bar menu of charcuterie and baguettes.

⊞ H9 ⊠ Woollahra Hotel, 116 Queen Street, Woollahra ☎ 9327 9713 ⏲ Daily lunch, dinner 🚌 389

BODEGA ($$)

bodegatapas.com

This spirited tapas restaurant is all Latin flavors, matadors on the walls, tattoos on the staff, rock'n'roll on the stereo and serious cheffing. Bodega is an award-winning restaurant—order the corn tamale or the 12-hour lamb and you'll see why.

⊞ D9 ⊠ 216 Commonwealth Street, Surry Hills ☎ 9212 7766 ⏲ Fri lunch, Tue–Sat dinner 🚌 423

DOLPHIN HOTEL ($$)

dolphinhotel.com.au

A Surry Hills institution, the Dolphin has evolved into a slick, wine-centric pub with an Italian menu. Book a table in the white-on-white fine dining room, order pizza, pasta or burgers in the public bar or on the terrace, or head to the wine room for antipasto.

⊞ E9 ⊠ 412 Crown Street, Surry Hills ☎ 9331 4800 ⏲ Mon–Sat 11.30am–midnight, Sun 11.30–10 🚌 423

FLAVOUR OF INDIA ($$)

flavourofindia.co

Sydney isn't particularly renowned for Indian restaurants, but this is one of the best. In business for almost 30 years,

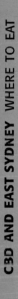

the dishes capture the cooking styles from every corner of the Indian sub-continent.

🔢 H8 ✉ 128 New South Head Road, Edgecliff ☎ 9326 2659 🕐 Daily dinner
🚇 Edgecliff

IPPUDO ($–$$)

ippudo.com.au

Popular eatery famed for high-quality, authentic *ramen* and melting pork buns. Lines can be long, but the bar serves Japanese craft beers while you wait.

🔢 D7 ✉ Level 5, Westfield Sydney, 188 Pitt Street ☎ 8078 7020 🕐 Mon–Wed 11–10, Thu–Sat 11–11, Sun 11–9 🚇 Town Hall

LONGRAIN ($$$)

longrain.com/sydney

Large, convivial communal tables, unusual cocktails and shared plates of inspired and madly flavorful Southeast Asian food have cemented the award-winning Longrain's position as one of Sydney's finest Asian diners.

🔢 D9 ✉ 85 Commonwealth Street, Surry Hills ☎ 9280 2888 🕐 Mon–Fri lunch, dinner daily 🚌 378

LUCIO'S ($$$)

lucios.com

Australian art, Northern Italian cuisine and top shelf service are the trademarks of this long-established restaurant. Seasonal ingredients are the order of the day.

🔢 G9 ✉ 47 Windsor Street, Paddington ☎ 9380 5996 🕐 Tue–Sat lunch, dinner 🚌 389

THE PAVILION ($$$)

pavilionrestaurant.com.au

Enjoy a lunch of refined Italian classics on the delightful terrace with quintessential Sydney vistas. The Pavilion Kiosk serves light meals, gourmet sandwiches, muffins and cakes to go or eat on the leafy deck with park views.

🔢 E6 ✉ 1 Art Gallery Road, The Domain ☎ 9232 1322 🕐 Daily 9–3, kiosk 8–4
🚇 St. James/Martin Place

RED LANTERN ($$$)

redlantern.com.au

Chef Luke Nguyen and Mark Jensen's award-winning Vietnamese restaurant is a glamorous, French Indochine-inspired dining space with a menu of flavor-packed regional Vietnamese dishes such as smoked duck rice paper rolls or salt and chilli squid. The tasting menus are a great snapshot.

🔢 E7 ✉ 60 Riley Street, Darlinghurst ☎ 9698 4355 🕐 Lunch Fri 12–3, Tue–Sun 6pm–late 🚌 373

SPICE I AM ($$)

spiceiam.com

The decor may be no-frills but the food is stellar—fiery, authentic Thai dishes that have drawn the locals for years. The fried snapper with green mango salad is a knock-out. More recently, they've established their own farm to grow the herbs and vegetables used in their dishes.

🔢 D8 ✉ 90 Wentworth Avenue, Surry Hills ☎ 9280 0928 🕐 Tue–Sun lunch, dinner
🚌 M10, 440

TETSUYA'S ($$$)

tetsuyas.com.au

One of Sydney's top chefs has transformed Japanese cuisine to an Australian artform. As winner of several prestigious awards, reservations at this restaurant are essential.

🔢 C8 ✉ 529 Kent Street ☎ 9267 2900 🕐 Sat lunch, Tue–Sat dinner 🚇 Town Hall
🚌 438

Farther Afield

Relax at the coastal holiday suburbs of Manly and Bondi or go for sports action at Olympic Park. Also on offer are day-trips to the nearby dramatic Blue Mountains, or a wine-tasting trip to the famed Hunter Valley.

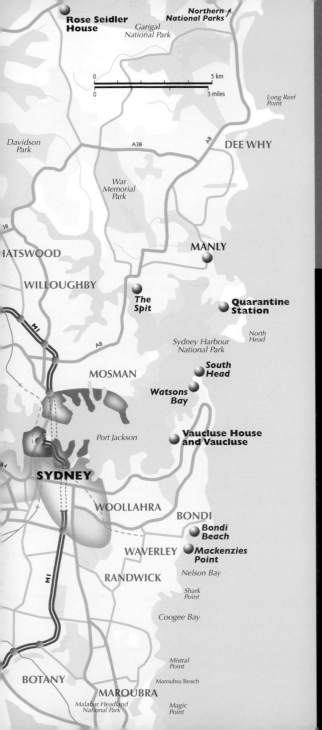

Rose Seidler House

Garigal National Park

Northern National Parks

0   5 km

0   3 miles

Long Reef Point

Davidson Park

A38

DEE WHY

A8

War Memorial Park

ATSWOOD

38

MANLY

WILLOUGHBY

The Spit

Quarantine Station

Sydney Harbour National Park

North Head

M1

MOSMAN

A8

South Head

Watsons Bay

Port Jackson

Vaucluse House and Vaucluse

SYDNEY

M1

WOOLLAHRA

BONDI

Bondi Beach

WAVERLEY

Mackenzies Point

Nelson Bay

RANDWICK

Shark Point

M1

Coogee Bay

Mistral Point

BOTANY

MAROUBRA

Malabar Headland National Park

Maroubra Beach

Magic Point

Bondi Beach

One of the world's most famous surfing beaches, Bondi, should not be missed

THE BASICS

bondivillage.com
- See map ▷ 93
- Bondi Beach
- Bondi Pavilion Community Cultural Centre 9083 8400
- Daily 24 hours
- Cafés and restaurants
- Bondi Junction, then bus 380, 382
- Bondi & Bay Explorer, 380, 382, 389
- Generally good
- Free
- Frequent festivals, exhibitions and events

HIGHLIGHTS

- Beach
- Cafés on Campbell Parade
- Exhibitions and events in Bondi Pavilion Community Cultural Centre
- Clifftop walk to Bronte Beach
- Golf overlooking the ocean
- Surfing
- Bondi Markets

Enjoy Sydney's outdoor life at this world-famous strip of surf and sand. Regardless of the season, join the locals as they swim, sunbathe, jog, eat, drink or simply stroll along the water's edge. This is the place for people-watching.

Bondi Beach Summer or winter, Bondi is quintessential Sydney. This is one of the world's most famous strips of surf, sand and beach life, and there is no better way of understanding how the locals enjoy themselves than to head down to Bondi. The Aboriginal name roughly means "the noise of tumbling waters," a description that sums up this beach and its rolling surf. Bondi is perfect for a summer sunbathing and surfing session, or a brisk winter walk along the clifftop path to Tamarama and Bronte beaches. Bondi is Sydney at its very best. In summer, you may see a surf carnival or other beach event, while the Bondi Pavilion Community Cultural Centre often holds musical and theatrical performances and art exhibitions.

Beachside Bondi street life is entertaining, with lots of bars, pubs and cafés, bookshops and surf and beach clothing shops. You can play golf overlooking the ocean at the public Bondi Golf Course. It's also a great place to stay. Every Saturday (9–1) and Sunday (10–4), the grounds of Bondi Beach Public School become the Bondi Markets (▷ 104), with designer clothing, handmade jewelry, arts, crafts, homeware and secondhand goods.

The ultimate chill-out destination—Manly is a top weekend spot for Sydneysiders

Manly

The slogan "seven miles from Sydney and a thousand miles from care" originated in the late 1880s, when ferries greatly shortened the journey to the popular suburb of Manly. Sydneysiders have flocked here ever since.

Manly The ocean beach at Manly is a spectacular setting for annual sporting events such as Ironman competitions, bicycle races, surf life-saving carnivals, as well as beach volleyball and swimming tournaments. In summer, Manly and its excellent beaches, such as Shelly—all just a short ferry ride from the city—draw surfers and swimmers, but there is plenty to do here at any time. The Manly Art Gallery and Museum has a good collection, and you can stroll around the modern Manly Wharf, which has more than 65 shops and cafés, and watch free street-entertainment. Continue to North Head and visit the historic Quarantine Station, or take a bus excursion to the wonderful northern beaches, such as Palm Beach or Mona Vale.

Crafty The outdoor Manly Market Place, every weekend 9–5, features vintage sellers, local crafts, fresh local produce and stalls selling baked treats and street food. Stretching along the pedestrian section of Sydney Road up to Whistler Street, it's the perfect interlude to a day at the beach and a great spot for souvenir shopping. Pick up some hand-crafted wooden Australian animals, leather goods, seaside paintings and organic skin-care products.

THE BASICS

hellomanly.com.au
⊞ See map ▷ 93
🕐 Daily 10–5.30
🚢 Manly
♿ Few
ℹ The Forecourt, Manly Wharf ☎ 9976 1430
🕐 Mon–Fri 9–5, Sat–Sun 10–4

HIGHLIGHTS

- Main beach and Shelly Beach
- Weekend Arts and Crafts Market
- Manly Art Gallery and Museum

Royal National Park

TOP 25

View from Stanwell Tops Lookout (left); a pleasant drive through the park (below)

THE BASICS

nationalparks.nsw.gov.au

🔷 Off map

✉ 2 Lady Carrington Drive, Royal National Park

☎ 9542 0648

🕐 Daily 7am–8.30pm (hours may vary due to weather)

🍴 Three cafés, picnic areas, BBQs

🚆 T4

🚌 D970

⛴ Bundeena

♿ Few

💰 Inexpensive

❓ Campgrounds

HIGHLIGHTS

- Cronulla esplanade
- Garie Beach
- Sandstone cliffs
- Mountain biking
- Whale watching
- Aboriginal history

The Royal National Park, the second-oldest national park in the world, is a heritage-listed wonderland of natural attractions with a diverse landscape running from beaches to bush to rainforest.

The park Established in 1879, this magnificent, sprawling national park covers more than 16,000ha (39,540 acres) of picturesque scenery from Port Hacking to Helensburgh, south of Sydney. It's rich in unique birds, flora and fauna, along with plenty of natural attractions and outdoorsy fun, from swimming, surfing, hiking and mountain biking to fishing, camping and picnicking. There are paddle boats for hire at the Audley Boatshed, and a range of Aboriginal sites and artifacts that you can learn about on a tour with an Aboriginal Discovery ranger. If you visit in spring, you'll see beautiful heathland wildflowers in bloom along the Coast track, the Curra Moors Loop track or the Wises track. Winter (Jun–Aug) is the best time for coastal scenery and whale watching. The multiple entry points to the park are well signposted, but pick up a map to locate attractions.

Cronulla This seaside town in southern Sydney, only 50 minutes by train from Central Station, is bustling yet laid back and beachy, with stretches of sand, shimmering rock pools, rolling parkland, cafés and restaurants. There are lots of surf schools, or you can catch a Cronulla Ferry for a discovery cruise. You can also try bushwalking in the park.

Sydney Olympic Park

The Olympic swimming pool, on the north side of the bridge

After hosting the "best Olympics ever," Sydneysiders embraced the Games site. But you will find more than Olympic memories here, and opportunities to participate in a sport of your choice.

Learn about sport The massive facility built for the Sydney 2000 Olympic Games has been transformed into a center for entertainment and sport. The best way to get here is by RiverCat ferry from Circular Quay. ANZ Stadium, the site of the Olympic opening and closing ceremonies and the focal point of the Sydney Olympic Park, now hosts major rugby and football (soccer) games. Guided tours run daily. The NSW Hall of Champions features photographs and memorabilia of athletes from the 1890s to the present. ANZ Stadium, in the Sydney Olympic Park, is the largest multi-use live entertainment and indoor sports arena in Australia.

Play sport Sydney Aquatic Centre has four world-class swimming pools. The complex also has spas, a sauna and steam room, a gym plus a children's water playground, high ropes adventure course and a café. Tennis World has courts for rent and offers individual coaching. The Indoor Sports NSW hosts concerts and exhibitions, and offers various ball games.

Bicentenial Park This green space comprises 40ha (99 acres) of parkland set in a wetland ecosystem. Facilities include barbecues, picnic shelters, trails, bicycle paths and an info point.

THE BASICS

sydneyolympicpark.com.au
✚ See map ▷ 92
✉ Homebush Bay
☎ Park: 9714 7888. ANZ Stadium: 8765 2000. NSW Hall of Champions & Sydney Showground: 9763 0111. Qudos Bank Arena: 8765 4321. Bicentennial Park: 9714 7888
🕐 Park daily 24 hours. ANZ Stadium: varies. NSW Hall of Champions: daily 9–5. Bicentennial Park: daily 6.30am–dusk
🍴 Various
🚆 Circular Quay/Central Station
⛴ Circular Quay
♿ Excellent
💵 Park free; other attractions prices vary
❓ Guided tours available

TIP

● Reserve your sports activities in advance.

HIGHLIGHTS

● Sydney Aquatic Centre
● ANZ Stadium
● NSW Hall of Champions
● Bicentennial Park

Vaucluse House and Vaucluse

HIGHLIGHTS

● The architecture
● Kitchen, drawing room and gardens
● Nielsen Park's beach and foreshore walk
● Parsley Bay

TIP

● Combine a trip to Vaucluse House with a seafood lunch at Doyles (▷ 106).

Visit this charming waterside mansion in the old eastern suburbs to admire its distinctive architecture and furnishings, then enjoy the well-tended gardens and art deco tearooms.

The house and grounds Much of modern-day Vaucluse, one of Sydney's most desirable water-side suburbs, was once part of the large estate of William Charles Wentworth. Set in 11ha (27 acres) of grounds, most of Gothic-style Vaucluse House was constructed in the 1830s for Wentworth, a prominent citizen, barrister and explorer (one of the first men to cross the Blue Mountains in 1813) and the father of the Australian Constitution. The house contains 15 rooms, furnished in the style of the mid-19th century, including an impressive entertaining

suite as well as a well-presented kitchen. The drawing room is splendid, with opulent fabrics and furnishings and a bay window framed by the shady veranda. Look out for the unusual corridor bedroom on the first floor—it is partitioned off from the hallway by a screen of cupboards. Little remains of the original estate, but the gardens and tearooms are delightful.

The best of Vaucluse This expensive suburb is full of large homes, leafy streets and waterside havens. Parsley Bay is a popular family beach, while the sand and gardens at Shark Beach and Nielsen Park are packed in summer. This latter beach is within Sydney Harbour National Park (▷ 28–29) and was once part of the Vaucluse estate. You can take a scenic walk, with great views, around the foreshore.

THE BASICS

sydneylivingmuseums.com.au

➕ See map ▷ 93

✉ Vaucluse House, Wentworth Road, Vaucluse

☎ 9388 7922

🕐 Wed–Sun 10–4

🍴 Tearooms

🚌 325

⛴ Watsons Bay (then bus 325)

♿ Inexpensive

❓ Tours and special events in the gardens

More to See

HUNTERS HILL

An attractive suburb and designated conservation area, Hunters Hill is worth visiting for the ferry ride west of the Harbour Bridge and to see the 1871 Vienna Cottage. This fine example of a small stone tradesman's house also has a small museum.

See map ▷ 92 ⊠ Vienna Cottage, 38 Alexandra Street ☎ 9817 2235 Museum 2nd and 4th Sun 2–4 Hunters Hill Free, Vienna Cottage inexpensive

KOALA PARK SANCTUARY

koalapark.com.au

In this private koala sanctuary you can cuddle koalas, hand-feed kangaroos and see traditional bush activities such as sheep shearing and boom-erang throwing. Check out the birds.

See map ▷ 92 ⊠ 84 Castle Hill Road, West Pennant Hills ☎ 9484 3141 Daily 9–5 Kiosk and picnic/barbecue area Pennant Hills, then buses 651–5 Expensive

MACKENZIES POINT

The wonderful views from this promontory extend to the beach at Bondi, out to the Pacific Ocean, and south down the rugged coastline.

See map ▷ 93 ⊠ South of Bondi Beach 24 hours 380, 382 Free

NORTHERN NATIONAL PARKS

nationalparks.nsw.gov.au

The greater Sydney region contains 10 national parks, as well as other natural reserves. In the north, you can visit Cattai, Lane Cove, Garigal and magnificent Ku-ring-gai Chase, but you need your own vehicle or take a tour to fully appreciate these superb wilderness areas.

Off map to north ☎ 9995 6500 Daily Kiosks and picnic areas Inexpensive

QUARANTINE STATION

qstation.com.au

Used since the 1830s to protect Sydney from smallpox, bubonic plague and other contagious diseases by quarantining migrants, the station is now an unusual museum.

Vienna Cottage at Hunters Hill

A resident of the Koala Park Sanctuary

You can see the burial grounds and rock engravings, while spooky night-time ghost tours come complete with tales of strange happenings.
🔲 See map ▷ 93 ✉ North Head, Manly ☎ 9466 1551 🕐 Tours daily 🚢 Manly, then bus 135 💶 Inexpensive

ROSE SEIDLER HOUSE

sydneylivingmuseums.com.au
Completed in 1950, this house was designed by one of Australia's leading Modernist architects, Harry Seidler. Its furniture comprises one of the most important post-war design collections in Australia.
🔲 See map ▷ 93 ✉ 71 Clissold Road, Wahnoonnga ☎ 9989 8020 🕐 Sun 10–4 🚆 Turramurra, then bus 575 to Cherrybrook Avenue 💶 Inexpensive

SOUTHERN NATIONAL PARKS

nationalparks.nsw.gov.au
The city's southern national parks—Kamay Botany Bay, the Royal, Georges River, Thirlmere Lakes and Heathcote—offer scenery ranging from freshwater lakes to beaches.

Your own transport is necessary, or contact Allambie Mini Buses.
🔲 Off map to south ☎ Parks: 9542 0666 🕐 Daily 🍴 Kiosks and picnic areas 💶 Inexpensive

SPIT TO MANLY WALK

This 8km (5-mile) harborside walk takes three to four hours, passing through bushland and the water-front suburbs surrounding Manly—great views of the Harbour and city.
🔲 See map ▷ 93 ✉ From the Spit Bridge, Middle Harbour ☎ 9247 5033 🍴 At Manly 🚌 178, 180, 182, 190 💶 Free

WATSONS BAY AND SOUTH HEAD

Watsons Bay was once a fishing hamlet and military base. This charming suburb has retained its village atmosphere. There are views of the water, swimming at Camp Cove and a walk to South Head in Sydney Harbour National Park.
🔲 See map ▷ 93 ☎ 9337 5511 🕐 Daily 🍴 Cafés and restaurants 🚌 324, 325 🚢 Watsons Bay 💶 Free

Take in the view on the walk to Manly

Excursions

BLUE MOUNTAINS

Sydneysiders, who have been flocking to the Blue Mountains since the early 19th century, come in summer for the cool mountain air, and in winter for invigorating walks and the fireside ambience of the guesthouses.

Cooler than Sydney in summer and bracingly cold in winter, the Blue Mountains are famous for their good hotels, excellent restaurants and grand scenery. People head to mountain towns like Springwood, Leura, Katoomba, Wentworth Falls, Blackheath and Mt. Victoria to take in the views, walk the trails, shop for arts, crafts and antiques and generally enjoy the mountain air. The Three Sisters, a unique rock formation, is a major tourist draw, as are the luxurious spas. A variety of superb temperate climate gardens are open for inspection, and the cool-climate annex of the Royal Botanic Garden Sydney at Mt. Tomah is brilliantly hued in the fall and a mass of flowers in spring and summer.

HAWKESBURY VALLEY

Visit the quiet hamlets and farms of the Hawkesbury Valley, or cruise the river on a ferry and learn about the region's convict past while taking in the stunning riverside bushland.

The food bowl and timber source for the young colony of Sydney in the 1790s, the Hawkesbury Valley remains a place of calm and beauty on the city's doorstep. More than 80 percent of the valley is a national park, and there is a rich colonial legacy of old architecture to inspect.

The Hawkesbury River is navigable from the historic town of Windsor to the charming riverside settlement of Brooklyn. Boat tours run from Windsor and Wisemans Ferry, or you can take a trip with the river postman on his weekday run. If you have more time, consider houseboat hire for a few days of idyllic river cruising, stopping along the way to visit the antique and craft stalls and boutique galleries, or take a tour of the nearby glow worm caves.

HUNTER VALLEY

Wine lovers make a pilgrimage to this fertile valley, just a couple of hours north of the CBD, to sample new vintages, enjoy country hospitality and relish a memorable dining experience in rural surroundings.

The historic Hunter Valley vineyards are three hours north of Sydney, near the old coal-mining town of Cessnock. Bus tours are available from Sydney and, given the nature of the main activity here, may be the preferred means of travel. A well-established circuit passes the cellar doors of dozens of wineries, where you are encouraged to sample the different products and may be invited to meet and observe the winemakers in their cellars. There are many fine restaurants in the area where you can buy a good meal accompanied by some excellent local wines. It's not just wine on the table here either—there are plenty of breweries and distilleries in the area.

THE BASICS

winecountry.com.au
Distance: 120km
(72 miles)
Journey Time: Bus trip
takes 3 hours
🚌 Bus from Sydney
ℹ️ Hunter Valley Tourist
Information 455 Wine
Country Drive, Pokolbin,
near Cessnock
☎ 4993 6700

SOUTHERN HIGHLANDS

Rural towns and villages with old-world charm, specialty shops, country estates with grand gardens, and cozy B&Bs set in pretty surroundings are all good reasons to head for the Southern Highlands.

Unwind in the Southern Highlands, a couple of hours' easy driving to the southwest of the city. The hospitality ranges from grand manors to small B&Bs, and the tariff often includes a hearty breakfast made from fresh produce. Arts and crafts outlets, antiques shops, bookshops and specialist food outlets are found in the charming towns and villages, with some top restaurants for fine dining and luxury spas for unwinding and pampering.

Mittagong is the regional retail hub, but the nearby town of Berrima has Australia's best-preserved Georgian architecture. Cricket fans can visit the Bradman Museum & International Cricket Hall of Fame in Bowral, while lovers of English garden styles will find plenty of choices.

THE BASICS

southern-highlands.
com.au
Distance: 130km
(81 miles)
Journey Time: Two
hours' drive southwest of
the CBD
ℹ️ Southern Highlands
Welcome Centre
☎ 1300 657 559

FARTHER AFIELD EXCURSIONS

Shopping

THE AUSTRALIAN GEOGRAPHIC SHOP

Operated by a popular magazine, this shop sells unusual and environmentally friendly Australian books, gifts and sturdy outdoor clothing.

➕ Off map ✉ Shop 1001, Westfield Shopping Centre, Bondi Junction ☎ 9257 0060 🚇 Bondi Junction

BERRIMA VILLAGE POTTERY

berrimavillagepottery.com.au

Sells a large range of functional and decorative pottery that is made on site, as well as beautiful homewares from around the world.

➕ Off map ✉ 8 Jellore Street, Berrima ☎ 4877 1987

BLUE MOUNTAINS CHOCOLATE COMPANY

bluemountainschocolate.com.au

Watch chocolate being made, take part in a chocolate-making course, enjoy free tastings, and choose from 60 different handmade chocolates.

➕ Off map ✉ 176 Lurline Street, Katoomba ☎ 4782 7071 🚇 Katoomba

BONDI MARKETS

bondimarkets.com.au

Every Sunday, stalls at this beachfront market fill up with arts, crafts, designer clothing, retro furniture and an interesting range of pre-owned goods.

➕ Off map ✉ Corner of Campbell Parade and Warners Avenue, Bondi Beach ☎ 9315 8988 🕐 Sun 10–4; Farmers' Market Sat 9–1 🚌 380, 382

THE BROOK

bluemountainsattractions.com.au/brook-art-a-crafts-co-op.html

Everything here has been handcrafted by local artists—prints, paintings, patchwork, jewelry, cards, soaps, stained glass and wooden toys. It's a cooperative business staffed by craft members.

➕ Off map ✉ 1a Ross Street, Glenbrook, Blue Mountains ☎ 4739 9511

PLAYA BY LUCY FOLK

Australian designer Lucy Folk's Bondi Beach branch is an inspired, soft coral-pink cloud where her earthy, relaxed apparel, sunglasses, jewelry, cosmetics, swimwear, hats and bags float alluringly.

➕ Off map ✉ Shop 3, 111–113 Hall Street, Bondi Beach 🕐 Mon, Wed, Fri–Sat 9–6, Thu 9–7, Sun 10–5 🚌 379

RIP CURL SURF SHOP

ripcurl.com.au

This iconic surf label provides everything you need for a great day surfing or just hanging out, including surfboards and all the latest gear.

➕ Off map ✉ 82 Campbell Parade, Bondi Beach ☎ 9130 2660 🚌 380, 382

TUCHUZY

tuchuzy.com

Ultra-chic designer fashion boutique with stylish imports and the best of Australian talent.

➕ Off map ✉ Shop 11, The Beach House, 178 Campbell Parade, Bondi Beach ☎ 9365 7775 🚌 380, 381, 382

DELICACIES

Australia really is gourmet country. Indigenous items like finger limes are a wild pop of flavor. Tropical fruits like mangoes abound, as does incredible Beechworth honey and olive oil like Toscana from the Grampians, and great cheese—try anything from Bruny Island in Tasmania. Farmers markets are a great snapshot of Australian delights.

Entertainment and Nightlife

AUSTRALIAN REPTILE PARK

reptilepark.com.au

Located at Gosford on the Central Coast less than an hour's drive north of Sydney, this place has reptiles of all kinds, including crocodiles, snakes and the wonderful Galapagos tortoises, which can weigh up to 180kg (400lb) and live for as long as 160 years. Also here are koalas, kangaroos, emus and parrots and Australia's only spider zoo, featuring Spider World and Tarantulaville—not for the fainthearted.

⊞ Off map ⊠ Pacific Highway, Somersby ☎ 4340 1022 🕐 Daily 9–5

CARRIAGEWORKS

carriageworks.com.au

This contemporary multi-arts center is housed in the old 19th-century Everleigh Rail Yards. Within its industrial environs, you can see live performances, installations, exhibitions and masterclasses, as well as a Saturday farmers' market.

⊞ Off map ⊠ 24 Wilson Street, Everleigh ☎ 8571 9099 🕐 Mon–Sat 10–6 🚆 423

CITY FARM CALMSLEY HILL

calmsleyhill.com.au

This is a great place for the family to experiences bush life, including shearing sheep, tractor rides and milking demonstrations. There's a café, a milk-bar-style take-out and lots of space to picnic—at tables or on the grass.

⊞ Off map ⊠ 31 Darling Street, Abbotsbury ☎ 9823 3222 🕐 Daily 9–4.30 🚉 Fairfield

CLOUD 9 BALLOON FLIGHTS

cloud9balloons.com.au

An adventurous way to view Sydney is from the air. Take a hot-air balloon flight and follow it with a champagne breakfast.

⊞ Off map ⊠ Annangrove ☎ 1300 555 711 🕐 Daily at dawn 🚉 Parramatta

HOTEL BONDI

hotelbondi.com.au

After a day on the beach, this is a great place to mix with the locals, listen to live bands, play pool or just hang out.

⊞ Off map ⊠ 178 Campbell Parade, Bondi Beach ☎ 9130 3271 🕐 Daily 🚌 380, 382

ROYAL RANDWICK RACECOURSE

australianturfclub.com.au

This famous racecourse offers more than 50 horse-racing meetings a year.

⊞ B10 ⊠ Alison Road, Randwick ☎ 9663 8400 🚌 372, 373, 374, 377

SEYMOUR CENTRE

seymourcentre.com.au

In the heart of Sydney University campus and home to three arts companies, this performing arts center has four performance venues, a spacious courtyard and restaurants and bars.

⊞ Off map ⊠ Corner of Cleveland Street and City Road, Chippendale ☎ 9351 7940 for performance information 🚉 Redfern 🚌 352, 370, 422, 428

WATER SPORTS

You can windsurf from Rose Bay (☎ 9371 7036), go diving at Coogee (☎ 9665 6333) or sail with the Northside Sailing School (☎ 9969 3972). Weekend surf carnivals, where lifesavers from opposing clubs compete, are held at beaches such as Bondi and Manly from October to March and you can watch competitive sailing on the water. The most exciting races, between 6m (19ft) long skiffs, are held on Saturday afternoons from mid-September to April—full details are available from the Sydney Flying Squadron (☎ 9955 8350).

Where to Eat

PRICES

Prices are approximate, based on a
3-course meal for one person.
$$$ over A$60
$$ A$40–A$60
$ under A$40

THE BACH EATERY ($$)

bacheatery.com.au

Championing local and New Zealand
produce, The Bach is a casual diner with
a clever, compact menu. Think Ora mar-
inated salmon or Cloudy Bay clams and
a glass of crisp white wine.

🗺 Off map 🖂 399 King Street, Newtown
☎ 8084 4093 🕙 Wed–Sat 5.30–late, Sun
12–3, 5.30–late 🚊 Newtown

BONDI TRATTORIA ($$)

bonditrattoria.com.au

This café-cum-restaurant provides
tempting Italian food and not-to-be-
missed views over Bondi Beach.

🗺 Off map 🖂 34 Campbell Parade, Bondi
Beach ☎ 9365 4303 🕙 Daily 7am–midnight
🚌 333, 300, 382

CATALINA ($$$)

catalinarosebay.com.au

This bright, breezy restaurant is one of
Sydney's finest, showcasing Australian
seafood and luscious cocktails.

🗺 Off map 🖂 Lyne Park, Rose Bay ☎ 9371
0555 🕙 Mon–Sat 12–12, Sun 12–6 🚌 324,
325

CONTINENTAL DELI BAR BISTRO ($$)

continentaldelicatessen.com.au

With a laidback, European style, the
Continental is a great place to sit at the
bar. Order a cheese and charcuterie
selection and sip on an exquisitely well-
crafted cocktail.

🗺 Off map 🖂 210 Australia Street, Newtown
☎ 8624 3131 🕙 Mon–Thu 12–11, Fri–Sat
12–11.45, Sun 12–10 🚊 Newtown

DOYLES ON THE BEACH ($$$)

doyles.com.au

Sydney's most famous seafood restaurant opened in 1885. It has great food
and wonderful harbor views.

🗺 Off map 🖂 11 Marine Parade, Watsons
Bay ☎ 9337 2007 🕙 Daily lunch, dinner
🚌 324, 325 ⛴ Watsons Bay

DUNBAR HOUSE ($$$)

dunbarhouse.com.au

Lovely restored colonial house with
beach and views of the Sydney skyline
from the terrace. Its chic daytime café
serves elegant offerings alfresco.

🗺 Off map 🖂 9 Marine Parade, Watsons
Bay ☎ 9337 1226 🕙 Daily breakfast, lunch
🚌 324, 325 ⛴ Watsons Bay

ICEBERGS DINING ROOM ($$$)

idrb.com

Icebergs is elegant and fashionable, with
Bondi sea views from the dining room,
bar and terrace. The food is regional
Italian and the menu seasonal.

🗺 Off map 🖂 1 Notts Avenue, Bondi Beach
☎ 9365 9000 🕙 Tue–Sun lunch, dinner
🚌 380, 382

AUSTRALIAN WINES

There have been vineyards in New South
Wales and other regions of the country
since the 1820s. Most of these produce
fine varieties such as Cabernet Sauvignon,
Shiraz, Chardonnay and Chablis. There are
hundreds of labels, but a few good wine-
makers to look out for include Lindemans,
Rosemount Estate, Houghtons, Wyndham
Estate, Henschke, Tyrrell's, Penfolds and
Wolf Blass.

Where to Stay

Sydney is a thriving business and tourism hotspot, and its accommodations options cater accordingly, from beachside getaways to serviced apartments and luxurious designer hotels.

Introduction

Sydney's diverse accommodations industry caters to all budgets. At the upper end there's the luxurious Four Seasons, set right on the water's edge, and the Westin Sydney, occupying the classic old post office building in Martin Place. At the lower-price end of the spectrum, the ever popular Cambridge Hotel offers good budget rooms with an excellent near-city location.

More Budget Choices
There are also many economical self-catering apartments, and reasonably priced guesthouses and hostels are plentiful. Bed-and-breakfasts are numerous, especially in the outer suburbs and rural areas close to the city.

Where to Stay
Sydney's major hotel areas can be found in the CBD, around Darling Harbour and Pyrmont, Circular Quay, Central Railway and the inner eastern suburbs.

Time it Right
Sydney is a popular destination all year round, but some events see tourist numbers swell massively, so it pays to do your research and book well in advance. Sydney's annual Gay and Lesbian Mardi Gras (mid February to early March) attracts hundreds of thousands of local and international visitors. Vivid Sydney (late May to mid-June) is a similarly popular festival of light, music and ideas. New Year's Eve is also a massive event, with fireworks lighting up the Harbour Bridge and attracting huge crowds.

STAY AT THE AIRPORT
Although Sydney's CBD is only 11km (7 miles) from the international airport, there are times when a stay at an airport hotel is necessary. Fortunately there are some good options: Ibis Budget Sydney Airport (☎ 8339 1840) is nearer the Domestic terminal; Rydges Sydney Airport (☎ 9313 2500) is within the International terminal, and the fun, designer Felix Hotel (☎ 8303 8888) is walkable from Domestic and a short drive to International.

From modern boutique hotels to Victorian guest-houses—it's all here in Sydney

Budget Hotels

AUSTRALIAN SUNRISE LODGE

australiansunriselodge.com

This has a good choice of single or double rooms, most with private balcony and bathrooms. It is well located in the vibrant suburb of Newtown, with 22 rooms.

➕ Off map ✉ 485 King Street, Newtown
☎ 9550 4999 🚉 Newtown 🚌 422

CREMORNE POINT MANOR

cremornepointmanor.com.au

On the north shore, this spacious 30-room manor house provides kitchens, laundry service, free WiFi and a continental breakfast.

➕ G3 ✉ 6 Cremorne Road, Cremorne Point
☎ 9953 7899 ⛴ Cremorne Point

IBIS BUDGET SYDNEY EAST

accorhotels.com

An economy hotel with 115 rooms close to transport and the lively Kings Cross nightlife. Some rooms cater to visitors with reduced mobility.

➕ F8 ✉ 191–201 William Street, Kings Cross
☎ 9326 0300 🚉 Kings Cross

THE MAISONETTE

sydneylodges.com

Conveniently located, The Maisonette is a heritage building on the outside, with contemporary guest rooms with a touch of vintage on the inside. Rooms include air conditioning, flat screen TVs and the choice of private or shared bathrooms. (Note: the three floors are accessed by stairs only.)

➕ F6 ✉ 31 Challis Avenue, Potts Point
☎ 9357 3878 🚉 Kings Cross

METRO ASPIRE HOTEL

metrohotels.com.au

In a quiet street but close to the action, the Metro Aspire has rooms decked out in executive style, with private balconies and bathrooms. There are family rooms and conference facilities.

➕ C8 ✉ 383–389 Bulwara Road, Ultimo
☎ 9221 1499 🚌 376, 391

SONG HOTEL SYDNEY

songhotels.com.au

This refreshed hotel has contemporary rooms with soundproof windows, free WiFi and smart TVs. You can opt for ensuite or shared bathrooms. Nine of the rooms are themed to celebrate prominent Australian women. You can also bid on room prices and save.

➕ D8 ✉ 5–11 Wentworth Avenue ☎ 9264 2451 🚉 Museum

VIBE HOTEL RUSHCUTTERS BAY

vibehotels.com/hotel/rushcutters-bay-sydney

Recently refurbished, with rooms enjoying a view of the rooftop pool, this hotel, close to the airport, is good value.

➕ G7 ✉ 100 Bayswater Road, Rushcutters Bay ☎ 13 84 23 🚌 200, 324, 325

BUDGET STAYS

In addition to many budget hotels, Sydney has dozens of good, inexpensive backpackers' lodges. Prices start at A$20 per night and many establishments offer reduced rates for long stays. Accommodations vary from private rooms to dormitories and the best backpacker areas are Kings Cross, inner-west Glebe and beach suburbs such as Bondi and Coogee. Another budget option is staying in a "hotel". In Australia, the word hotel has two definitions: it can mean either a conventional hotel or a pub with rooms.

Mid-Range Hotels

PRICES

Expect to pay between A$150 and A$300 per night for a double room in a mid-range hotel.

1888 OVOLO

1888hotel.com.au

An art-filled boutique hotel in a restored wool store with exposed brick, original beams and luxury bathrooms. Rooms have a New York loft vibe, and some are split level. Book direct for generous freebies such as breakfast, mini bar, happy hour and superfast WiFi.

➕ B7 ✉ 139 Murray Street, Pyrmont ☎ 8586 1888 Ⓖ Tram Light Rail to Pyrmont 📁 Darling Harbour

CAMBRIDGE HOTEL

cambridgehotel.com.au

This friendly, 149-room hotel is close to Oxford Street, within walking distance of the CBD and with good transport links. There's a spa and a heated pool. The rustic Italian restaurant serves breakfast and dinner every day.

➕ E8 ✉ 121 Riley Street, Surry Hills ☎ 9212 1111 Ⓖ Central 📁 370, 380

THE CARRINGTON HOTEL

thecarrington.com.au

Named in 1886 after Lord Carrington, a former Governor of New South Wales, this grand hotel in the Blue Mountains is National Trust listed. It offers all mod cons, fine dining, a grand high tea every Sunday and a spa.

➕ Off map ✉ 15–47 Katoomba Street, Katoomba ☎ 4782 111 🚉 Katoomba

HARBOUR ROCKS HOTEL

mgallery.com

In a cleverly restored historic building at the heart of The Rocks, this hotel is ideally located for exploring top Sydney sights. The 59 rooms are decorated in heritage colors, there's a good restaurant, friendly bar and fitness center.

➕ D4 ✉ 34 Harrington Street, The Rocks ☎ 8220 9999 Ⓖ Circular Quay

HOTEL RAVESIS

hotelravesis.com

This boutique hotel with 12 tastefully decorated and furnished rooms and suites, has views over Bondi Beach. There is a restaurant and cocktail bar.

➕ Off map ✉ 118 Campbell Parade, Bondi Beach ☎ 9365 4422 📁 380, 382

THE KIRKETON HOTEL

kirketon.com.au

This small, cool hotel in a heritage-listed building features rooms in shades of chocolate and charcoal, a good Asian restaurant and an award-winning underground cocktail bar.

➕ F8 ✉ 229 Darlinghurst Road, Darlinghurst ☎ 9332 2011 🚉 Kings Cross

THE MACLEAY

themacleay.com

If you want hotel convenience with a touch of home, these sleek serviced studio apartments, some with Harbour views, are an excellent choice. They have well-equipped kitchenettes, are air conditioned and come with free WiFi.

APARTMENTS

Apartment-style hotels in Sydney generally fall into the mid-range price category. These so-called serviced apartments vary from one to three bedrooms, with separate dining areas and kitchens or kitchenettes. Most larger apartments have private laundry facilities, and many are large enough for families or small groups.

➕ F7 ✉ 28 Macleay Street, Potts Point
☎ 9357 7755 🚉 Kings Cross

MEDUSA HOTEL

medusa.com.au

This award-winning boutique hotel in a three-story mansion is one for design and style buffs. With just 17 stylish rooms, some with ornate balconies, set around a central courtyard, this is an oasis in the heart of Darlinghurst, between William Street and Oxford Street. It's also just a 5-minute walk from Kings Cross train station.

➕ F8 ✉ 267 Darlinghurst Road, Darlinghurst
☎ 9331 1000 🚌 352, 377

METRO APARTMENTS ON DARLING HARBOUR

metrohotels.com.au

Enjoy the excellent view of Darling Harbour from these roomy apartments, in two adjacent buildings on the west side of the city. They include fully serviced one-bedroom suites and apartments. King Street has 10 apartments, a rooftop pool and barbecue facilities; Sussex Street has 30 apartments. All sleep up to four people and have a balcony, fully equipped kitchen, laundry facilities, living and dining area, shower and bath.

➕ C7 ✉ 132–136 Sussex Street ☎ 9199 2517 🚉 Town Hall

QUALITY HOTEL CKS SYDNEY AIRPORT

airportinn.com.au

Close to the Domestic and International terminals and with a shuttle bus service, this property provides comfortable, convenient accommodations, a restaurant and unlimited high-speed WiFi.

➕ Off map ✉ 35 Levey Street, Arncliffe
☎ 9556 1555 🚉 Wolli Creek

THE RUSSELL

therussell.com.au

This delightful Victorian building has been renovated to provide boutique-style accommodations. The sitting room and its bar, furnished in period style, open on to a balcony over George Street, and there is a rooftop garden. Breakfast is served downstairs in the Fortune of War, Sydney's oldest pub.

➕ D4 ✉ 143A George Street, The Rocks
☎ 9241 3543 🚉 Circular Quay

SPICERS GUESTHOUSE

spicersretreats.com

This upscale guesthouse in the heart of Hunter Valley is surrounded by lush, beautiful gardens and features a contemporary Italian restaurant, Eremo. The minimalist decor is serene and luxurious, both in the rooms and the Cottage, a short stroll from reception.

➕ Off map ✉ Ekerts Road, Pokolbin, Hunter Valley ☎ 4993 8999

THE YORK BY SWISS-BELHOTEL

theyorkapartments.com.au

These 120 suites and residences are close to Darling Harbour and the CBD. Suites range from studio to two-bedroomed executive apartments, with a kitchen, bathroom, laundry and balcony.

➕ D6 ✉ 5 York Street ☎ 9210 5000
🚉 Wynyard

LOCATION

As with all large cities, you may need to be flexible when choosing your hotel location. While CBD hotels are close to rail and bus services, those around Circular Quay and The Rocks also enjoy proximity to ferry services. Accommodations in the eastern suburbs have rail and bus connections and are often set in pleasant, quiet locations.

Luxury Hotels

FOUR SEASONS HOTEL

fourseasons.com

The Four Seasons, with 531 rooms and overlooking Sydney Harbour and its iconic bridge, has a pampering spa, pool and fitness center. Australian produce is celebrated in the bright cuisine at Mode Kitchen & Bar, while Grain, their award winning bar, showcases more than 200 whiskies.

🔲 D5 ✉ 199 George Street ☎ 9250 3100 🚇 Circular Quay

HYATT REGENCY SYDNEY

hyatt.com

This premium, waterside hotel is Sydney's largest, with 892 modern, sophisticated rooms over 24 gleaming floors. Dining options include the outdoor rooftop Zephyr, the Sailmaker restaurant and the Lobby Lounge. It's perfect for business and equally good for leisure, with stunning views and the exclusive Regency Club Lounge.

🔲 C7 ✉ 161 Sussex Street ☎ 8099 1234 🚇 Town Hall 🚢 Sydney Aquarium

INTERCONTINENTAL SYDNEY

icsydney.com.au

Close to the Botanic Gardens and The Rocks, this 503-room hotel is based on the historic 1851 Treasury Building. The Café Opera features sumptuous buffets with an emphasis on seafood, while La Cortile is a history-soaked lounge offering high tea and a cocktail hour. Dine alfresco amid the hotel's historic sandstone arcades.

🔲 D5 ✉ 117 Macquarie Street ☎ 9253 9190 7095 🚇 Circular Quay

LILIANFELS RESORT & SPA

lilianfels.com.au

This luxurious haven, nestled in the verdant Blue Mountains, has tennis courts, two heated pools and opulently decorated rooms. The renowned and elegant Darley's restaurant serves Modern Australian cuisine.

🔲 Off map ✉ Lilianfels Avenue, Echo Point, Katoomba ☎ 4780 1200 🚉 Katoomba

QT HOTEL

qthotelsandresorts.com

The 200 rooms in this eclectic boutique hotel built within the historic Gowings and State Theatre buildings are perfect for design fans who like something quirky. There's a day spa and good onsite dining, and rooms come with free WiFi and oversized soaking tubs.

🔲 D7 ✉ 49 Market Street, Sydney ☎ 8262 0000 🚇 St. James

SHANGRI-LA HOTEL SYDNEY

shangri-la.com

With spectacular views of Sydney Opera House and Sydney Harbour Bridge, this elegant hotel features 565 rooms, a day spa, three restaurants and one incredible bar with fantastic views.

🔲 D5 ✉ 176 Cumberland Street, The Rocks ☎ 9250 6000 🚇 Circular Quay

SHERATON GRAND HOTEL SYDNEY HYDE PARK

marriott.com

Situated just opposite pretty Hyde Park, this 558-room hotel, with its grand three-floor lobby, includes a rooftop health club and a heated indoor pool with city views. The modern rooms are decked out in dusky, neutral tones and come with coffee-makers and WiFi.

🔲 D7 ✉ 161 Elizabeth Street ☎ 9286 6000 🚇 St. James

Need to Know

Sydney is the tourist capital of Australia, and the more you plan your trip, the more you'll get out of it. Use these pages to familiarize yourself with travel options and gain useful insider knowledge of the city.

Planning Ahead

When to Go

Sydney's tourist months are December to February. March and April or September and October are better times to visit, as the crowds have thinned and the weather is warm and sunny. It is advisable to take an umbrella as subtropical thunderstorms are common.

TIME

Sydney is 9 hours ahead of the UK, 14 hours ahead of New York and 17 hours ahead of Los Angeles.

AVERAGE DAILY MAXIMUM TEMPERATURES

JAN	FEB	MAR	APR	MAY	JUN	JUL	AUG	SEP	OCT	NOV	DEC
79°F	79°F	77°F	72°F	66°F	63°F	61°F	64°F	68°F	72°F	75°F	77°F
26°C	26°C	25°C	22°C	19°C	17°C	16°C	18°C	20°C	22°C	24°C	25°C

Spring (September to November) is warm with sunny days that are mostly dry; the nights are cool to mild.

Summer (December to February) is warm to very hot but can also be humid and rather wet. Thunderstorms are common.

Fall (March to May) sees mild to warm days with mild to cool nights. This season is generally dry.

Winter (June to August) is mostly dry with mild, sunny days and cool nights. Take a medium-weight coat.

WHAT'S ON

January *Sydney Festival:* A three-week long cultural celebration.
International cricket matches: Sydney Cricket Ground.
Australia Day (26 Jan): A public holiday with fireworks and festivals.
February *Chinese New Year:* Fireworks and feasting in Chinatown.
Tropfest: Outdoor short-film festival.
February/March *Gay and Lesbian Mardi Gras:* The city's biggest street parade.
March/April *The Golden Slipper:* A horse race.

Anzac Day (25 Apr): War Veterans Parade.
Royal Easter Show: Agriculture show, Sydney Showground.
May *Sydney Writers' Festival:* National and international speakers.
June *Sydney Film Festival:* Films from many nations.
August *City2Surf:* A 14km (9-mile) run to Bondi Beach.
September/October *Rugby Grand Finals:* League and union teams battle it out in their respective finals.
October *Manly Jazz Festival:* Music by the sea.

November *Neighbourhood Festivals:* Double Bay and Newtown, stalls, music.
December *Sydney to Hobart Race* (26 Dec): Start of one of the world's great yacht races.

Listings Pick up a free copy of *Timeout Sydney* for the full span of entertainment listings. Friday's *Sydney Morning Herald's* Shortlist and the *Daily Telegraph's* Planner on Saturdays are also good resources. Also check out the City of Sydney's What's On site, as well as sydney.com/events.

Sydney Online

At the heart of Australia's digital culture, Sydney has excellent websites with information on everything from the cinema to local news, weather and listings of hotels and restaurants.

sydney.com
The official Sydney website. A complete guide with travel information, and listings of hotels and events in the city.

sydneyoperahouse.com
Look here for listings of performances and events at the Sydney Opera House—a must-see for everyone—with a booking option and a virtual tour.

discoversydney.com.au
General information for Sydney. Includes what to see and do, where to eat, shop and stay.

sydneyairport.com.au
Flight information and all you need to know at the airport including hotels and shopping.

smh.com.au
The *Sydney Morning Herald's* website gives up-to-date information on dining, nightlife and events news.

broadsheet.com.au/Sydney
A cultural wrap-up of what's going on, from new cafés to pop-up sales, exhibitions and road trips

visitnsw.com
What to see and do in New South Wales, including top destinations, visitor information centers and accommodations.

au.timeout.com/sydney
The go-to site for food and drink reviews and what's on day and night in Sydney.

concreteplayground.com/Sydney
The latest in restaurant and bar reviews.

Getting There

ENTRY REQUIREMENTS

All visitors to Australia require a valid passport and an Electronic Travel Authority (ETA), which has replaced the traditional visa.

A Tourist ETA is valid for multiple travel within one year (or the expiry date of your passport, if sooner) on three-month visits. Visa applications can be submitted online at homeaffairs. gov.au and are generally approved quickly.

Australia does not allow entry if your passport expires within six months of your entry date.

BEFORE YOU GO

● Vaccination certificates are not normally required, unless you have visited an infected country within the previous 14 days.

● Tourism Australia: Mailbox 358, 2029 Century Park E Ste. 3150, Los Angeles, CA 90067
☎ 310 695 3200

AIRPORT

Sydney International Airport is the main port of entry for travelers arriving by air. There are numerous daily flights, buses and train services to Sydney from all major towns and cities in Australia.

24km (15 miles) · 16km (10 miles) · 8km (5 miles) · Sydney · Sydney International Airport

ARRIVING BY AIR

Sydney Airport (tel 9667 9111; sydneyairport. com.au) at Mascot, south of the city, is the main port of entry for overseas visitors on direct flights. The airport, a short distance from Sydney's CBD, also handles the majority of domestic passenger arrivals. There are taxis and ride shares, a rail service, bus services, car rental outlets and shuttle buses that loop around major hotels and accommodation areas.

Sydney trains take 13 minutes from the airport to central Sydney and run every 10 minutes. The cost is around A$17.20 and you'll need to buy an Opal card and put credit on it first. They are available at multiple points and cover a very wide network.

A taxi from the airport into the city takes 20–40 minutes (depending on traffic) and costs around A$50.

ARRIVING BY BUS

Bus travel is often more expensive than flying, but buses are nevertheless one of the best ways to see more of Australia on your way

to Sydney. Country and interstate buses pick up and depart from the Transit Centre at the Eddy Avenue side of Central Station. Daylight and overnight buses arrive each day from Melbourne and Brisbane and usually take between 8 and 12 hours respectively. The main interstate carrier is Greyhound Australia (tel 1300 473 946; greyhound.com.au).

ARRIVING BY CAR
Car rental is inexpensive in Australia and is a popular way for families to save money on inter-capital travel. The main highways between cities are excellent. Sydney and larger regional hubs have several car rental firms, offering a variety of vehicles and deals. You must be at least 25 years old, and you can pay additional fees to have the insurance excess waived. The main rental companies are Avis, Budget, Europcar, Hertz, National and Thrifty.

ARRIVING BY SEA
This is not the most common means by which to arrive in Sydney, although the city is a very popular port for cruise liners. Celebrity Cruises, Holland America, Royal Caribbean, Princess Cruises and many more include Sydney on their cruise schedules. Sydney's Overseas Passenger Terminal, at Circular Quay, services cruise ships.

ARRIVING BY TRAIN
Regional and Intercity trains (tel 132 232; transportnsw.info) travel to and around New South Wales and offer a comfortable way to see the state and the country. The Trainlink trains arrive at Central Station, part of the metropolitan train system's underground City Loop service. The XPT train service from Melbourne to Sydney takes around 10–11 hours. The Indian Pacific, running from Sydney to Perth via Adelaide, connects two oceans in one of the world's longest train journeys. Enjoy the sights from your cabin, and take a range of optional off-train sightseeing tours along the way.

INSURANCE
Check your policy and buy any necessary supplements. It is vital that travel insurance covers medical expenses, in addition to accident, trip cancellation, baggage loss and theft. Check the policy covers any continuing treatment for a chronic condition.

VISITORS WITH DISABILITIES
Most of Sydney's attractions are suitable for visitors using a wheelchair, with ramped public buildings and accessible buses, ferries, rail stations and taxis. (Note that Sydney is a very hilly city.) Some hotels have roll-in showers, and some have Braille signage. For details, check out sydneyforall.com.au and easyaccessaustralia.com.au/sydney.

Older buildings are often retrofitted with ramped access and many National Trust properties are at least partially accessible. Many Sydney attractions have hearing loops. You'll usually find parking places for drivers with disabilities, although you'll need a temporary permit from the Roads and Maritime Services to use them (☎ 13 2213).

Getting Around

DRIVING

- Sydney's traffic can be notoriously busy. The Waze app can divert you around congestion.
- Driving is on the left and overtaking traffic (which has the right of way) is on the right. This may not be immediately obvious on multilane highways, where the preference seems to be to stay in the right hand lane. On some stretches of winding roads there are lay-bys for slow traffic to let other drivers overtake.
- Take special care when driving on unsurfaced roads; they are best avoided. Avoid driving in the country at night. Beware of stray animals on motorways at dawn and dusk.
- Some road signs are peculiar to Australia, but most will be immediately understandable to visitors.
- Full details of Australia's road rules are available at aaa.asn.au.
- Speed limits are 50/60kph (31/37mph) in urban areas and 100/110kph (62/68mph) elsewhere unless indicated.
- Seatbelts must be worn in front and back seats.
- Fuel (unleaded and super unleaded) is sold by the liter.
- The legal limit for alcohol is 0.05 percent blood alcohol level.

Sydney is compact and much of it can be explored on foot, but taxis are plentiful. The city has a good transit system of buses and ferries, as well as a partly underground city and suburban rail system (tel 131 500) and an extended light rail currently under construction. Free public transport maps are available from bus, ferry and train offices at Circular Quay, Wynyard bus station and Town Hall train station.

The efficient Airport Rail Link (airportlink.com. au) runs from the International and Domestic terminals at Sydney Airport to the City Circle train line, stopping at Central, Museum, St. James, Circular Quay, Wynyard and Town Hall stations. Trains run about every 10 minutes and the complete trip takes around 20 minutes.

BY BUS

Sydney's buses are blue and white. The most important bus stations are Circular Quay (to Bondi Beach, the eastern suburbs, the south and some inner-west areas) and Wynyard (over Harbour Bridge). A smart card system operates across Sydney's public transportation network—the Opal card. When boarding a bus, train or ferry you need to tap the card against an Opal card reader and tap again (and listen for the "ding" tone indicating it has registered) when leaving at the end of your journey. The display screen shows the fare deducted and any value left on the card. The daily travel cost is capped at A$15.80 (adults, A$7.90 child/youth), A$2.70 on Sundays.

Sydney and Bondi Explorer (theaustralian explorer.com.au) are hop on-hop off, open-top city and beach tour buses. A one-day ticket costs A$55 (adult), family pass A$148. These double-decker buses offer great views of the city from the top deck. You can either take the red route for the Sydney tour (first service 8.30am) or the blue route (first service 9.30am) which goes to Bondi. Both take in some major sites, and your tickets are valid for 24 hours, so you can do both tours.

BY BOAT

Ferry services operate from four wharves on Circular Quay to 30 places around Sydney Harbour, including Manly and Taronga Zoo, and up-river to Homebush Bay and Parramatta. Buy tickets from the Circular Quay counters, Wharf 4 or use an Opal card. Water taxis operate along the Harbour; Yellow Water Taxis are the main operator (tel 9299 0199).

BY CAR

You must be over 25 to rent a car and have a home country or international driver's license. Compulsory third-party insurance is included in rental prices, which are on average A$70–A$100 per day. Major Sydney car-rental companies include: Avis (tel 136 333); Budget (tel 1300 362 848); Hertz (tel 133 039).

BY TAXI OR RIDE SHARE

Cabs and ride shares like Uber are abundant in Sydney and you can generally hail cabs on the street or call on 13CABS (tel 132227). Zero200 (tel 8332 0200) specialize in wheelchair-friendly taxis.

BY TRAIN

A light rail service connects Central Station to Chinatown, Darling Harbour, Star City casino and the Sydney Fish Market. A new extension of the light rail is slated for completion in 2019. Sydney's inner-city rail services include the City Circle (Central, Town Hall, Wynyard, Circular Quay, St. James and Museum) and Eastern Suburbs Line, which runs from Central to Town Hall, Martin Place, Kings Cross, Edgecliff and Bondi Junction. Off-peak tickets (weekends and weekdays after 9am) offer a 45 percent saving.

FURTHER INFORMATION

● For timetable and transportation ticket information, call 131 500 (daily 6am–10pm).
● Trainlink train information, call 132 232
● Useful websites: opal.com.au; sydneybuses.info; sydneytrains.info.

TAXI

Essential Facts

MONEY

The Australian unit of currency is the Australian dollar (A$), comprising 100 cents (¢). Banknotes come in denominations of 100, 50, 20, 10 and 5 dollars. Coins come in 5, 10, 20 and 50 cents (silver), and 1 and 2 dollars (gold-colored).

ELECTRICITY

The electricity supply in Australia is 230–250 volts AC. Three-flat-pin plugs are the standard (although note that they are unlike British plugs). Hotels provide standard 110-volt and 240-volt shaver sockets.

EMERGENCY PHONE NUMBERS

● Police, ambulance or fire: 000 (24 hours). All calls for these services are free.
● Dental, pharmaceutical, personal, or other: See the front of the A–K volume of the Sydney White Pages telephone book (whitepages.com.au)

MEDICAL TREATMENT

● Medical, dental and ambulance services are excellent but costly.
● Doctors and dentists are readily available and there are many medical facilities where appointments are not necessary.
● For after-hours medical assistance, call 13SICK (tel 13 7425).

MEDICINES

You may bring in prescribed medications. Keep them in the original containers and bring a copy of your doctor's prescription to avoid problems at customs.

NEWSPAPERS AND MAGAZINES

● The main national newspaper is *The Australian*.
● The major city newspaper is the *Sydney Morning Herald*.
● For business, financial and investment news see *The Australian Financial Review*.

OPENING HOURS

● Shops: generally Mon–Fri 9–5.30, Sat 9–4. Late-night shopping until 9 on Thu. Large stores open Sun until 4. Suburban corner shops often open daily 8–8 or later.
● Post offices: Mon–Fri 9–5. Sydney GPO hours are Mon–Fri 8.15–5.30, Sat 8.30–2.

● Banks: Mon–Thu 9.30–4, Fri 9.30–5. City head-office banks open Mon–Fri 8.15–5.

POSTAL SERVICES
● Larger post offices provide services such as passport and ID photos, money transfers and foreign currency.
● Stamps can be purchased from hotels, and from some newsstands and souvenir shops.
● For postage information, call 131318.

PUBLIC HOLIDAYS
1 Jan, 26 Jan (Australia Day), Good Fri, Easter Mon, 25 Apr (Anzac Day), 2nd Mon in Jun (Queen's birthday), 1st Mon in Aug (NSW; banks only), 1st Mon in Oct (Labour Day: NSW state holiday), 25–26 Dec. School summer holidays are mid-December to late January. As a result transportation and tourist facilities are busy and accommodation is heavily reserved.

SENSIBLE PRECAUTIONS
● Report theft or any other incident to your hotel and/or the police as soon as possible. If your traveler's checks are stolen, advise the relevant organization.
● The non-emergency police inquiries number is 9281 0000.
● Sydney's police wear blue uniforms and a peaked cap or baseball cap. They are generally helpful and polite.
● Tap water is safe to drink; the only medical problems you are likely to experience are sunburn and mosquito bites.
● The Australian sun is strong, so always apply a high SPF sunblock, wear sunglasses, a broad-brimmed hat and long sleeves, and avoid the summer sun from 11 to 3.
● Dangerous currents and marine stingers can cause problems in the sea in summer, so take notice of lifeguards and any beach signs.
● Women are generally safe in Sydney, but walking alone in parks or on beaches at night and traveling alone on trains out of the central city area is not recommended.

CUSTOMS REGULATIONS
● Visitors aged 18 or over may bring in 25 cigarettes or 25g of tobacco or cigars; 2.25 liters of alcohol; plus other dutiable goods to the value of A$900 per person.
● There's no limit on money imported for personal use. Amounts in excess of A$10,000 or its equivalent must be declared on arrival.
● Animals are subject to quarantine, and goods of plant or animal origin must be declared on arrival. It is forbidden to bring in food.
● Drug smuggling is treated very seriously and harshly. Importing firearms and products from endangered species is illegal or restricted.

STUDENTS
Australia is popular with students. The country has an extensive array of inexpensive hostel and backpacker accommodations, and travel options include bus, rail and air services that are not too expensive if booked well in advance. Students can supplement their income by a range of part-time work. Be sure to apply online for a Working Holiday visa (homeaffairs. gov.au) before you enter the country.

CASH AND CREDIT CARDS

Currency exchanges at hotels, some shops, tourist areas and outlets such as American Express and Thomas Cook are open outside banking hours. Airport exchange facilities are open daily 5.30am–11pm. You can obtain cash from 24-hour cash machines (ATMs) throughout the city and country. Major credit cards (American Express, Visa and MasterCard) are widely accepted. A 10 percent goods and services tax is automatically added to your purchase. However, if you buy goods valued at A$300 or more from any one supplier you can claim the tax back from the designated booths at Sydney Airport.

CONSULATES

- Canada ☎ 9364 3000
- France ☎ 9268 2400
- Germany ☎ 8302 4900
- Portugal ☎ 9262 2199
- Spain ☎ 9261 2433
- UK ☎ 9247 7521
- USA ☎ 9373 9200

TELEPHONES

- Public telephones are found at phone booths, post offices, hotels, service stations, shops, rail and bus stations and cafés. Local calls cost 50¢ for unlimited time (most Australian coins or phone cards can be used).
- Long-distance calls within Australia, known as STD, vary in price. Calls are less expensive after 6pm and all day Sunday.
- Operator assistance and directory assistance: 1223 (Australia), 1225 (International).
- Reverse-charge (collect) calls: 12 550.
- Phonecards come in values of A$2 to A$20; credit cards can also be used from some (silver) phones. International calling cards, available at newsagents, can cut the cost of international calls.
- For international (IDD) calls (can be made from some public phones), dial 0011 followed by the country codes: US and Canada 1; UK 44; France 33; Germany 49.
- To call Australia from the US, dial 011 61; from the UK, dial 00 61, then drop the initial zero from the area code.
- To call a Sydney number from outside the metropolitan area, use the prefix 02

TELEVISION AND RADIO

- ABC (Australian Broadcasting Corporation) and SBS (Special Broadcasting Service) have no commercials.
- Sydney has three commercial stations: Channels 7, 9 and 10, plus multiple digital channels.
- Cable and streaming services are available in most major hotels.
- Sydney has many commercial radio stations and a network of community radio stations. The ABC runs a national public radio network, which includes Classic FM, Double J and Radio National, a news and information station.

TOILETS

Free in parks, public places, museums, department stores and bus and train stations.

Language

Most people understand the greeting "G'day" as being Australian slang for "hello." But there are lots of other less familiar words and phrases that you're likely to encounter on a trip to Australia. Australians sometimes say several words as one "waddayareckon" ("what do you reckon?") and "owyagoin" ("how are you going?"). Listed here are the meanings of some of the words and phrases you'll most likely hear.

AUSSIE ENGLISH

ankle biter	small or young child	knock off	steal something, a counterfeit product
arvo	afternoon		
barney	argument, fight	larrikin	lout, mischievous
big smoke	the city	pommie	English person
bloke	man	rack off	go away, get lost
bonza	excellent, attractive	sheila	girl, woman
		skite	boast, brag
bush	the country	slab	carton of 24 beer cans
chinwag	chat, conversation		
		struth!	exclamation of surprise
cobber	mate, friend		
dag	person with little dress sense, uncouth	stubby	small bottle of beer
		sunnies	sunglasses
drongo	slow-witted person	tee up	to organize something
dunny	outside toilet	tinnie	can of beer
fair dinkum	genuine, true	true blue	genuine
full as a boot	intoxicated	tucker	food
get stuffed	go away	yarn	story
hard yakka	hard work	yonks	long period of time
hooroo	goodbye		

Timeline

THE FIRST FLEET

The unusual birth of modern Australia might so easily have been a disastrous false start, but Sydney and the nation have thrived, thanks initially to Governor Phillip and the people who traveled on the First Fleet of 11 ships from England. These reluctant pioneers of 1788—including 568 male and 191 female convicts, and 200 marines and their wives and children—suffered incredible hardships to set this isolated colony on its feet. For the first two years, lack of farming skills meant near starvation, and it was only the fortuitous arrival of supply ships from England that saved the day.

40,000–50,000BC Aborigines arrive from Southeast Asia.

AD1770 Captain James Cook and the crew of the *Endeavour* arrive at Botany Bay.

1779 Suggestions are made in England that New South Wales could become a penal colony.

1787 The First Fleet sails from Portsmouth, England. The 11 ships carry more than 1,400 people.

1788 The First Fleet arrives at Botany Bay. The commander and first governor of the colony, Captain Arthur Phillip, deems the site unsuitable and moves his settlement north to Port Jackson (Sydney Harbour). The colony of New South Wales is proclaimed.

1793 The first free settlers land in Sydney.

1804 An uprising of 400 Irish convicts occurs at Castle Hill. Australia's second settlement is founded at Hobart, Tasmania.

1813 A route over the previously impenetrable Blue Mountains is finally discovered by explorers Wentworth, Lawson and Blaxland, opening up Australia's agricultural potential.

1832 Assisted passages over the next 140 years help millions of people, mainly Britons, to emigrate to Australia.

The Endeavour *sailing towards Tahiti in 1769, en route for Australia (left); panoramic view of Sydney Harbour (middle); International Aquatic Centre, home to the 2000 Olympic swimming competitions (right)*

1840 Convict transportation to New South Wales ends.

1851 Gold is discovered near Bathurst, and Sydney's population doubles in 10 years.

1901 The Commonwealth of Australia is proclaimed at Centennial Park on 1 January, joining the six Australian colonies into a federation.

1914–18 and 1939–45 Australian troops fight overseas during World War I and II.

1947 Post-war immigration from Europe begins, boosting skilled workers.

1999 Australia votes against becoming a republic.

2000 Sydney hosts the Olympic Games.

2003 Australian troops join US forces in the war on Iraq.

2013 Severe bush fires wreak devastation in the Blue Mountains and across NSW.

2015 Australia hosts the soccer AFC Asian Cup—the first country outside of Asia to do so.

2017 Australia legalizes same-sex marriage.

2018 Australia's population reaches 24 million, with 5 million living in Sydney.

GOLD FEVER

Although declared a city in 1842, it was not until the 1851 discovery of gold near Bathurst, beyond the Blue Mountains, that Sydney really came of age. Word soon spread and prospectors arrived from all over the world. Sydney boomed, and its population virtually doubled in a decade.

Index

Sydney 25 Best

WRITTEN BY Anne Matthews and Rod Ritchie
UPDATED BY Jane Ormond
SERIES EDITOR Clare Ashton
COVER DESIGN Jessica Gonzalez
DESIGN WORK Liz Baldin
COLOR REPROGRAPHICS Ian Little

Published in the United Kingdom by AA Publishing.

ISBN 978-1-6409-7206-3

SEVENTH EDITION

Printed and bound in China by 1010 Printing Group Limited

10 9 8 7 6 5 4 3 2 1

A05671
Maps in this title produced from mapping © MAIRDUMONT / Falk Verlag 2018 and data available from openstreetmap.org © under the Open Database License found at opendatacommons.org
Transport map © Communicarta Ltd, UK

We would like to thank the following photographers, companies and picture libraries for their assistance in the preparation of this book.

2–18t Courtesy of Tourism New South Wales Online Image Library; 4tl AA/M Langford; 5 AA/P Kenward; 6cl © The Royal Botanic Gardens & Domain Trust; 6cc AA/ M Langford; 6cr AA/S Day; 6bl AA/J Tims; 6bc Jeff Greenberg 5 of 6/Alamy Stock Photo; 6br AA/ M Langford; 7cl AA/M Langford; 7cc AA/S Day; 7cr AA/S Day; 7bl AA/S Day; 7bc AA/S Day; 7br Photodisc; 10c Destination NSW; 10/1t AA/M Langford; 10/1c James Horan/Destination NSW; 10/1b Courtesy of Tourism New South Wales Online Image Library; 11c AA/M Langford; 12b Courtesy of Tourism New South Wales Online Image Library; 13t AA/M Langford; 13c AA/P Kenward; 13b AA/P Kenward; 14tr AA/M Langford; 14tcr AA/P Kenward; 14bcr AA/M Langford; 14br AA/P Kenward; 16tr AA/T Kelly; 16cr AA/P Kenward; 16b AA/M Langford; 17tl Courtesy of The Australian Museum; 17tcl AA/J Wyand; 17bcl AA/M Langford; 17bl AA/C Osborne; 18tr James Horan/Destination NSW; 18tcr AA/P Kenward; 18bcr AA/S Day; 18br AA/M Moody; 19t AA/M Langford; 19tc AA/M Langford; 19c © CandyAppleRed Images/Alamy Stock Photo; 19bc AA/S Day; 19b AA/M Langford; 20/1 AA/M Langford; 24l AA/M Langford; 24/5t © The Royal Botanic Gardens & Domain Trust; 25r © The Royal Botanic Gardens & Domain Trust; 26l AA/M Langford; 26r AA/S Day; 27 AA/M Langford; 28l AA/S Day; 28r AA/S Day; 28/9 AA/P Kenward; 29t Courtesy of Tourism New South Wales Online Image Library; 29bl AA/S Day; 29br Courtesy of Tourism New South Wales Online Image Library; 30l AA/S Day; 30tr AA Australia Tourist Commission; 30/1 AA/M Langford; 31r AA/M Moody; 32l Destination NSW; 32r AA/M Moody; 33 AA/S Day; 34t AA/S Day; 34b Destination NSW; 35 AA/A Baker; 36t AA/M Langford; 36b AA/P Kenward; 37 AA/M Langford; 40l Courtesy of the Museum of Contemporary Art, Sydney; 40r Courtesy of Tourism New South Wales Online Image Library; 40/1 Courtesy of the Museum of Contemporary Art, Sydney; 41t AA/S Day; 41bl Courtesy of the Museum of Contemporary Art, Sydney; 41br Courtesy of the Museum of Contemporary Art, Sydney; 42l Courtesy of HISTORIC HOUSES TRUST OF NEW SOUTH WALES; 42r Courtesy of HISTORIC HOUSES TRUST OF NEW SOUTH WALES; 43 AA/M Langford; 44 Destination NSW; 45tr AA/S Day; 45cr AA/S Day; 46t AA/S Day; 46bl Courtesy of Tourism New South Wales Online Image Library; 46br Peter Murphy; 47 AA/S Day; 48 Courtesy of Tourism New South Wales Online Image Library; 49 Destination NSW; 50t Destination NSW; 50c AA/M Langford; 51t–52t AA/P Kenward; 53 © Roger Donovan/Alamy Stock Photo; 56 Destination NSW; 57tr Courtesy of Tourism New South Wales Online Image Library; 57cr Courtesy of Tourism New South Wales Online Image Library; 58l AA/S Day; 58r AA/M Langford; 59l AA/P Kenward; 59r AA/P Kenward; 60l © Bart Pro/Alamy Stock Photo; 61 © Jon Lord/Alamy Stock Photo; 62t AA/S Day; 62bl James Horan/Destination NSW; 62br James Horan/Destination NSW; 63 Destination NSW; 64 AA/M Langford; 65 James Horan/Destination NSW; 66 AA/P Kenward; 67 AA/P Kenward; 70 Art Gallery New South Wales; 71tr Art Gallery of New South Wales; 71cr AA/P Kenward; 72t Courtesy of Australian Museum; 72bl Photo Stuart Humphreys © Australian Museum; 72br Courtesy of Australian Museum; 72/3 Courtesy of Australian Museum; 73t Courtesy of Australian Museum; 73bl Courtesy of Australian Museum; 73br Courtesy of Australian Museum; 74 AA/P Kenward; 74r AA/M Langford; 75l Courtesy of Tourism New South Wales Online Image Library; 75r Courtesy of Tourism New South Wales Online Image Library; 76 AA/S Day; 76/7t Destination NSW; 76/7c Destination NSW; 77t AA/S Day; 77cr Destination NSW; 78l AA/P Kenward; 78r Courtesy of Tourism New South Wales Online Image Library; 79t–82t AA/S Day; 79bl AA/S Day; 79br AA/S Day; 80bl AA/M Langford; 80br AA/M Langford; 81bl AA/M Langford; 81br AA/S Day; 82bl State Library, NSW; 82br AA/M Langford; 83 AA/S Day; 84t–86t AA/M Langford; 87-88 AA/M Langford; 89–90 AA/P Kenward; 91 Destination NSW; 94l AA/M Langford; 94r AA/M Langford; 95l Courtesy of Tourism New South Wales Online Image Library; 95r AA/P Kenward; 96l Destination NSW; 96r Tourism Wollongong; 97t AA/P Kenward; 98/9t AA/P Kenward; 98bl Courtesy of HISTORIC HOUSES TRUST OF NEW SOUTH WALES; 98br Courtesy of HISTORIC HOUSES TRUST OF NEW SOUTH WALES; 99bl Courtesy of HISTORIC HOUSES TRUST OF NEW SOUTH WALES; 99r Courtesy of HISTORIC HOUSES TRUST OF NEW SOUTH WALES; 100/1 AA/S Day; 100bl AA/P Kenward; 100br AA/P Kenward; 101 Courtesy of Tourism New South Wales Online Image Library; 102/3 AA/P Kenward; 104 Destination NSW; 105 AA/M Langford; 106 AA/P Kenward; 107 Destination NSW; 108/9t AA/C Sawyer; 108tr Hotel Ravesis; 108tc AA/P Kenward; 108bcr AA/M Langford; 108br Shangri-La Hotel, Sydney; 110/1 AA/C Sawyer; 112 AA/C Sawyer; 113 Destination NSW; 114–123 AA/M Langford; 124bl AA; 124/5b AA; 125br AA/S Day.

Every effort has been made to trace the copyright holders, and we apologize in advance for any accidental errors. We would be happy to apply the corrections in the following edition of this publication.

Titles in

D0496496